PASTORAL
CARE
UNDER THE
CROSS

God in the Midst of Suffering

Richard C. Eyer

SAINT LOUIS

Copyright © 1994 Concordia Publishing House
3558 S. Jefferson Avenue, St. Louis, MO 63118-3968
Manufactured in the United States of America

Library of Congress Cataloging-in-Publication Data.

Eyer, Richard C. 1939–
    Pastoral care under the cross: God in the midst of suffering/
    Richard C. Eyer.
    Includes bibliographical references.
    ISBN 0-570-04643-2
    1. Church work with the sick. 2. Church work with the terminaly ill. 3. Suffering—Religious aspects—Christianity. 4. Pastoral counseling. I.Title.
    BV4335.E94   1994
    253-dc20   94-34466
                                                    CIP

---

1 2 3 4 5 6 7 8 9 10   03 02 01 00 99 98 97 96 95 94

To Richard John Neuhaus,
friend and faithful pastor,
whose voice in the marketplace
has been an encouragement
to my ministry

Contents

Preface

I have wanted to write this book for many years, but the time was not right for it until now. I needed to get to the point where I could look back long enough to evaluate my ministry (as much as anyone can honestly do such a thing). There are two reasons why I wanted to write this book. First, I needed to sum up for myself the nearly 20 years I have spent in chaplaincy. Second, I needed the discipline of putting thought into much of what had been intuitive to me. I felt I had done the right thing with patients many times, but was not sure I had thought much about it at the moment of doing it. This book, therefore, has forced me to think about what I have done in the particular area of pastoral care of people who are ill and dying.

The theme throughout this book is what Martin Luther has called "the theology of the cross." He identifies these words as conveying the substance of God's way of caring for us, and Luther encourages pastors to follow this example. "He deserves to be called a theologian," he writes, "who comprehends the visible and manifest things of God through suffering and the cross" and stresses that "God wished to be recognized in suffering."[1] Throughout this book, whether explicitly or implicitly, I have drawn my understanding of pastoral care from these words, the theology of the cross.

This is intended to be a book about how to interpret life's experiences of suffering in the light of the cross. In particular, the theology of the cross is an answer to the helplessness and loss of control which comes with illness and dying. The theology of the cross reminds us that it is through weakness and suffering that God comes to us most clearly, first on the cross and then in our experiences of suffering. It is important that pastoral care be understood in this theologically substantive way, and that whatever personal style a pastor may develop, he reflect this substance.

PREFACE

This is a book about one chaplain's way of doing ministry. If I have done something well or suggested a better way, it will be evident in those who model my attempts. I think I am as much a teacher as I am a care giver to the patients I have seen. Much of my teaching has been an attempt to counteract the shallow values of our culture that have avoided the truth about ourselves before God in times of crisis and in dying. It is my hope that whatever introspection, intuition, and experience I have had will be an encouragement to others in their ministry.

I am writing especially to pastors, but others may also benefit from this book: Christian men and women such as deaconesses, nurses, doctors, social workers, and all who bear one another's burdens in the name of Jesus Christ. The pastors I write to are addressed in the masculine, since that is the ancient tradition and the theology of the church with which I identify myself.

In the beginning of each chapter in Part 1, I offer a poem which, although not perhaps the best poetry, was written at my desk after visiting with a patient who inspired it. It has been a way throughout the years of chaplaincy for me to channel my feelings into something edifying. Until now, none of these poems has ever been shared with anyone other than my wife.

There are some people I want to thank for helping me write this book. Hal Senkbeil, friend and partner in the theology of the cross, has reminded me constantly of the need for emphasis on the Sacraments as part of my writing. Ed Veith, "professor" and affirming critic, kept me aware of the style and clarity of what I was writing. The three of us met twice a month to read to each other for criticism the things we hoped to publish. And I am thankful for Mary Alice Houghton, psychiatrist, who constructively criticized my chapter on Mental Illness and Pastoral Care. Thanks also to Julie Heun and Barb Bergquist, my coordinators, who typed and retyped this manuscript with alacrity and patience. Finally, I owe most thanks to my wife, Susan, who brought meals to my desk as I wrote, created an atmosphere conducive to writing, and listened interminably to my thinking aloud of much of what I wanted to say in print. The patients and staff of Columbia Hospital also deserve gratitude for their teaching me to be a pastor.

PART 1
The Context of Pastoral Care Today

Introduction

Fluids on the floor ... spilled from a Styrofoam cup ...
no, urine ...
A man asks, "Why can't I ... "
the question falters, the head drops,
he stares down blankly ... he drools ...
Bread, a wafer ... offered, eagerly accepted ...
Wine, drunk quickly ...
"All my life, from a child, God ... "
he stares, he drools, his head drops.
As if wind whistling through a partially open
window ... he breathes ... lungs filled ...
"What I don't understand is ... "
And I promise, "You are loved, forgiven ... "
He drools, "But ... "
"I am with you always!" He stares ..., "Ah, that's
the problem. No one stays ... here ... with me."
He stares, I promise, I leave,
he nods, he stares down.

NEW-AGE OFFERS OF PASTORAL CARE

Pastoral care has been understood traditionally to be the uninvited
spiritual nurturing of those suffering some kind of helplessness and
loss of control over life. It is modeled after God's care of us following Eden, and it has been God's way with us ever since, even to
the cross, where God sacrificed himself to heal us for time and eternity. But this Biblical notion of the cure of souls and the spiritual
care of others is a far cry from popular ideas of what today can
only be called secular spiritual care. In this phenomenon the thin
line between psychology and traditional spiritual care is crossed,
creating a hybrid which results in a pop psychology that is far more
secular than what Christians understand as spiritual.

13

I want to be clear to distinguish pop psychology from the medical specialty of clinical psychiatry. Clinical psychiatry may be helpful to the Christian who is learning to understand his own behavior. Seeing things in himself more clearly, he may be more likely to make confession of his sins and find absolution for the cure of his soul and the healing of relationships with others. In contrast, pop psychology offers easy answers of a quasispiritual nature aimed merely at making people feel good about themselves regardless of deeper ills. Because deeper ills remain unresolved, the soul remains ill, and self-care turns into preoccupation with self rather than moving the self to care for others. The concern of today's secular spiritual care is not the cure of souls but the cure of boredom, lack of success, or low self-esteem often generated by unresolved inner conflicts. One such attempt at providing spiritual care advertises a weekend of therapy inviting people to "spiritual unfoldment and total well-being"[1] for those burdened by "overeating, partying, and unmanageable body, stress, and going from one relationship to another."[2] Such secular spiritual care moves away from unsightly sick and dying people to youth-hungry, overindulgent specimens who want it all. Christians are indeed called to practice good stewardship of body and soul, exercising healthy discipline of the body and practicing a devotional life centered on the Word of God, but preoccupation with self can also become an end in itself divorced from service to God. Then "self-care" is transformed into idolatry. It is hardly a surprise that these who are caught up in secular spiritual care find little time to provide spiritual care of the sick and dying in the traditional Christian sense.

PSYCHOLOGY AND THE SPIRITUAL

This self-indulgent stress on feeling good as the goal of spiritual care has been coming for generations. The rise of psychology in the early part of the 20th century turned us in on ourselves. Although self-examination and attention to the inner person is nothing new to Christians, what was new was the preoccupation with the self without God. Psychology had paralleled the Christian faith from the time of the Greeks, but even the Greeks managed to make room for the gods. In contrast, the early days of Freudian psychiatry did not allow for God, and the church rejected such atheism. But in the 20 years I have worked with psychiatrists I have seen a return to finding a place for the spiritual.

It is not yet clear, however, what this blend of the spiritual and the psychological is all about, but the struggle to define it has been going on for most of this century. In my clinical training for chaplaincy there was a continual tug-of-war between those proposing a "clinical" (psychology) model of care and those convinced of a "pastoral" (spiritual) model. I believe there is always the temptation to leave the sufferer preoccupied with his own resources rather than to help him focus on God. There is a subtle urging in our culture and especially for those like myself in the medical environment to gain credibility and acceptance by thinking in psychological rather than spiritual terms.

I remember my own struggles with this seduction. A patient I was visiting in my student days suddenly interrupted our visit with, "Are you a psychologist?" My supervisor assured me that it was a compliment, but I was not long pleased with the identity that made me anything less than a pastor doing pastoral, not psychological, care. Shortly after CPE I wrote an article[3] that called attention to the "psychologizing of faith and life." In it I said there has been a subtle shift from the spiritual to the psychological, so that we no longer see ourselves as God sees us but as the psychologist sees us. When a man is charged with a senseless, violent crime, he is not thought of first as a sinner but as disturbed or mentally ill. And although he may be both, we hardly think of his behavior as evil. More likely we think of him only as antisocial or perhaps the victim of abusive parenting. Likewise, much secular spiritual care now begins not with a "sinner in the hands of an angry God" but with anxiety in the hands of a pop psychology guru. Confession is replaced by deep breathing, and moral teaching is superseded by self-expression. But this is not new to us; it is all grandfathered in under the heritage of early American individualism, relativism, and utilitarianism.

"Isms" That Offer Care

When I was speaking at a pro-life group about our responsibility as Christians to bear one another's burdens, a man in the audience from the Philippines talked with me during the break and asked for clarification. He said, "I don't understand what you mean. You talk about caring for the elderly and not abandoning them. In my country the elderly are highly respected and no one would think of abandoning them." He was having a hard time understanding what our culture calls "individualism," where everyone is an individual first and a member of society second, where self-sacrifice of any kind is a vanishing value. In some parts of the world it is the reverse. It needs to be recognized that individualism in our culture is killing us. It is pulling us away from each other, and even naive, faithful Christians often seek personal spiritual thrills more than spiritual care of one another.

One of the most disturbing experiences our hospital ethics committee faced was of adult children saying, "We'd like you to help us find a way to end our mother's life." She had been critically ill in the hospital for two months, and they were sick of it. Although she was not dying, having decided it was time she did, they first stopped to make funeral arrangements with their pastor and then met with the ethics committee. Too busy with their own lives to have time for their ailing mother, they had decided to shake off the burden of caring for her. This is the context in which we as pastors are called to give pastoral care. But if pastors have to contend with such self-centered individualism, they also have to contend with its companion, relativism.

Relativism is that great leveler and peacemaker that makes all things equal in a pluralistic society. If all things are relative and therefore equal, then no objective truth exists. In caring for the helpless, relativism pronounces that there is no right or wrong in decision-making at the end of life. Instead, everyone's personal choice matters most. The abortion debate of the past decades has been stalled by relativism. Pro-life people have not succeeded in convincing pro-choice people that abortion is wrong, because pro-life supporters assume an absolute morality, while the pro-choice argument is based on a relative morality that makes "choice" a higher value than the "sacredness of life."

INTRODUCTION

It is not difficult to see how spiritual care is distorted by relativism. If all is relative, then no one idea, method, or even assumed truth in spiritual care of others has any convincing claim on our lives. Enter the pastor who comes uninvited yet called by God to speak not only comfort but also truth to a suffering person. The pastor's words will be regarded as one option among many. I once visited a hospital patient who could not understand why she was suffering. We talked of God working through suffering to make himself known to us as a compassionate God who shares our suffering by way of the cross. Neither accepting nor rejecting, she responded, "That's an interesting idea." But apparently not a very convincing one, even though it's the only truth there is. It reminded me of Paul's debate on Mars hill with the curiosity seekers of Athens. This is the context in which faithful pastors attempt to do pastoral care today. As if individualism and relativism were not enough, we must also contend with a third component of culture: utilitarianism.

Utilitarianism is the "bottom line" of our culture. It teaches that if something works, it is good and valid. A twin to relativism, it doesn't care whether something is right or true but whether it does the job. Years ago I expressed criticism of an evangelism program our church body was promoting. After hours of debate with the head of an evangelism committee, he broke off the communication saying, "Well, all I can tell you is that it works." And that's the bottom line that seems to justify all things spiritual as well as material. If baptizing stillborns makes parents feel better, then "just do it." If calling the chaplain in when all else fails seems to comfort the patient, then "just do it." Utilitarianism isn't a hostile value; it doesn't mean to deny truth as relativism does. It just doesn't concern itself with those things. Parishioners expect their pastors to visit them in the hospital, not always because patients hope for an enlightening word but just because pastors get paid to do that sort of thing. Actually, many parishioners measure a pastor's visit to the hospital on the basis of whether or not they feel better afterwards. A patient told one of my lay-minister volunteers, "Well, I don't think I feel any better because of your visit, but thanks for coming anyway." This is today's utilitarian context. In this context God calls faithful pastors to offer pastoral care.

THE NEED FOR PASTORAL CARE TODAY

In the first sentence of this book I defined pastoral care as the "uninvited spiritual nurturing" that a pastor provides. It is uninvited in the sense that the person needing pastoral care often does not request it. In another sense, however, it never is uninvited because God, through the church, ordains pastors and calls them to nurture those who are hurting. Sometimes hurting people understand this better than pastors do. Bob and Marge, as they shake hands with their pastor after worship, announce that Bob will be entering the hospital on Wednesday. Nothing more is said; no overt invitation given. It is understood that the pastor and other members of the believing community will take the initiative to be there for them at that time. Or a death occurs, and the grieving expect the pastor to be an ongoing part of their spiritual nurture. Such expectations may be hard for pastors to accept, but they live out God's grace that comes uninvited into all of our lives.

What differentiates pastoral care from pastoral counseling (and makes it more difficult) is that in pastoral counseling the person in need initiates contact with the pastor and bears the burden of responsibility for what happens. In pastoral care the pastor bears the burden of responsibility for the encounter, at least initially, until the parishioner also sees a need to pay attention to his suffering. In pastoral counseling the pastor must develop the skills of a good counselor. In pastoral care the pastor must have a heart for the suffering that also enables him to suffer with the parishioner. When the day ends, I find that I am exhilarated by the pastoral counseling I have done and exhausted by the pastoral care I have given.

From Feelings to Holy Perspective

In the first sentence of this book I also said that we need to understand suffering in the context of "helplessness and loss of control over one's life." Someone has said that the willingness to live with our own helplessness may well turn out to be called faith. That does not make living with helplessness any easier, but it does put helplessness into holy perspective, a useful beginning for both pastor and parishioner. It is this encounter with helplessness and loss of control that makes pastoral care so exhausting. Not only the parishioner feels helpless and without control, but the pastor walks with the suffering parishioner through the valley of the shadow also feeling the helplessness, having no quick fix, but only a God who promises to be with them.

In a society saturated with feelings and increasingly unable to think clearly, the challenge for pastoral care is to move the sufferer from feelings of helplessness to a holy perspective. Holy perspective is that interpretation arrived at by pastor and suffering parishioner which is both sensitive to feelings and looks beyond feelings to Truth. Truth is not merely what pastor or parishioner feels personally but what God says to us in Jesus Christ, the meaning of which is revealed in the written Word. While some reject the Bible as irrelevant to life, saying that a first-century book cannot answer this century's questions, we have to ask whether our century is asking the right questions. It is still at the foot of the cross that we begin to learn what the right questions and answers are for our lives. Pastoral care is needed today more than ever before because it not only comforts but also models God's nurturing of us and God's invitation to us to nurture others. In an individualistic, relativistic, and utilitarian world, Scripture is light in the darkness. It moves people beyond self-care to the care of others. It moves people from feelings to a holy perspective on life.

Feelings are a legitimate part of what it means to be human, but feelings are not faith. For example, it would be hazardous to say that the experience of depression is due to loss of faith. Martin Luther suffered fits of melancholy but never lost his faith. In fact, it was in such moments of seeming despair that he held more closely the objective conviction that, though the devil told him he was lost and without God, Martin would shout from the foot of the cross that Jesus lives—and, therefore, in him, Martin lives.

Feelings are not faith but rather clues that identify needs. Pastoral sensitivity must include the willingness to feel another person's pain in order to know what that person needs. I tell my students in pastoral care that, when you are with a patient and begin to recognize a particular feeling arising in you, ask yourself where that feeling is coming from. It is a good bet that it is coming from the patient who touches off similar feelings in you. A patient or parishioner feeling frustration or impatience or fear will offer some of it to the pastor who is willing to listen carefully to this suffering parishioner. Feeling what another person feels is called empathy: sensitivity so keen that the listener begins to take on the feelings the speaker is conveying. The task of pastoral care is to accept these conveyed feelings without being swallowed up by them. Furthermore, pastoral care is to speak to these feelings with truth that rises above them, giving the patient or parishioner something to hang onto besides the feelings of a spiritual high. In this sense pastoral care ultimately teaches—compassionately—as well as comforts. In order to interpret God's presence and action in the lives of people, the pastor must pay attention to feelings. But to stop at shared feelings is to offer only momentary relief. Some interpretation of what has been shared must follow. Pastoral care requires both sensitivity and objectivity, so that feelings lead to the discovery of spiritual meaning. This is the challenge of pastoral care.

Pastoral Care as Support

Ultimately pastoral care offers support (spiritual sustenance) to a hurting person while God works in that person. We believe that what God is doing is good. Our ministry offers neither fatalism nor mere resignation, but rather conviction that God knows better than we do what is good for us, as we acknowledge when we pray, "Thy will be done." Praying "Thy will be done" is not so much to resign oneself to God's will as it is to plead for God's will to be done because we ourselves no longer know what is good and what is not. Because God's will is good and gracious, we don't have to know or name the outcome or the good, but can turn to God who names it for us and does what is good.

The medical profession (including psychiatry) as an institution of our culture cannot be expected to see pastoral care as anything other than one more support service for patients. That is perhaps as it should be, since culture ought not and cannot identify the spiritual needs of people. But within the culture, even in spite of it, individual people can. People in the medical profession can recognize pastoral care as something more than one more support service among many, especially those whose faith, frail or strong as it may be, gives them eyes to see God as Maker and Sustainer of people's bodies, minds, and souls. Nevertheless, there will be those who value the pastor as a support to patients (at least to the pastor's own parishioners) without knowing what it is they value. That is acceptable, given a nonfaith perspective in an imperfect world. We should be appreciative of that much understanding, but we pastors should not seek to discover our legitimacy in the medical profession's acknowledgment of our value to the patient. Acknowledged or not, our legitimacy comes from God, who invites us into the suffering one's life.

Probably every hospital chaplain, if not every parish pastor, realizes that the majority of people associate pastoral care with the event of dying. "If all else fails, call the pastor/chaplain." That phrase has for some time been the instinctive response of health care workers who see any value in the parish pastor or chaplain's contribution. I recall being alone on the hospital elevator with a man on his way to visit a patient. He remained silent throughout our ascent from the first floor to the fifth. As the elevator doors opened and he stepped out, he turned to me and said in wry seriousness, "I hope if I am ever a patient here I never have to see you." And too many times to count, one doctor in particular has stopped me in the hall to say, "Mr. (fill in the patient's name) has (fill in the number) hours to live; I'd like to have you prepare him to meet his Maker."

Although perhaps less than 10 percent of what I do as a hospital chaplain each day has to do with the moment of a patient's dying, it is a legitimate assumption that awareness of our mortality is to be associated with pastoral care. Individuals need to "make their peace with God," and they need community so that dying takes place in the context of reconciliation with both Christ and his church: the people of God. None of us lives to himself or dies to himself, but we do both in the presence of God and with those whom he has already made alive as his saints on earth and in heaven.

The need for pastoral care parallels the need for community. "It is not good that the man should be alone" applies to the sick and dying as much as to marriage. In a society that values autonomy as the highest good and the right to privacy as the greatest asset, even to ask for companionship at the time of one's helplessness and loss of control over life is sometimes unthinkable. But it is the task of the pastor, if necessary, to think of it for the parishioner. One such occasion demonstrated to me that the contribution of pastoral care is unique and beyond the scope of all other care.

A STORY OF PASTORAL CARE

Ann had been hospitalized three days, yet no one seemed to understand why she continued to weep day and night. Her rheumatologist had admitted her for joint pain and for long-standing arthritis that once again raged uncontrolled, but no analgesics seemed to help. Ann realized that the pain differed from anything she had ever experienced before. A psychiatrist had placed her on antidepressants, but it could be weeks before they worked their benefit. So, someone on the unit suggested that, since nothing else seemed to help, perhaps they should call the chaplain.

I found Ann in tears. She was bewildered and embarrassed by them, claiming to feel foolish because she could think of no reason to justify them. In the course of our visit I explored with her the death of her husband nine years before. With tears now absent and with keen recollection she told me about his suicide. She had found him hanging in the garage. Having experienced grief with many patients and sensing her absence of any feelings about this event, I asked if she had shed tears at the time of his death. She said no and did not elaborate. I took a stab at her curt response, suspecting it contained hidden anger. "Were you angry with him for what he did?" She quickly replied, "No, I loved him too much to be angry with him." Since Christians have most difficulty admitting anger, I asked her, "What if he had not taken his own life, but had just walked out on you? Would you then have been angry at him?" At this point she hesitated, her face reddened and her eyes welled up with tears. "Yes!" she cried out. "That's what he did to me and my daughter." Now instead of tears, there was a flood of verbal anger ... anger reflecting the ambivalence of love and hate she felt for her husband. We talked for an hour. Her tears disappeared. Her anger spent itself. In the end we prayed. In the prayer, as I always try to do, I included what we had just experienced in the way of God's healing of deep hurt and the need she had discovered to forgive her husband for what he had done to her and her daughter. The visit ended and I left.

Late the next day Ann left word for me to visit again. She enlarged the story of her rapidly healing grief by telling me that after years of alienation from her daughter due to the anger the suicide generated in both of them, they had been reconciled. She wanted me to know that I had been the catalyst for God's healing to transform her.

Pastoral care moves beyond the scope of psychology, since psychology cannot direct us to forgiveness received from the One who alone heals us completely. Pastoral care is unique. It does not derive its substance from the culture nor its legitimacy from the medical profession. Pastors need to lead the culture, not follow it, in providing the "one thing needful," which our Lord provides to and through us: forgiveness, hope, and a future for this life and the next. It is my hope that what follows in this book will help you learn to do that.

1

The Cross as Paradigm for Pastoral Care

A Human Body: My Crucifix

A human body, in front of me, dead.
All year long, before my morning eyes
    to remind me, remind me of the way life is.

A human body, on wood, nailed, hanging.
A strange sight, always there, when I'm not
    to keep me straight about the way things are.

A human body, so cold and lifeless, dead.
As alive a memory as ever there was
    to balance my seeing the horrors in a new light.

A human body, a mystery that sends life from death.
Answer to my hopeless fear and pain
    to crack the window of my life with hope.

A human body, still ... alive, quiet ... rejoicing with me.
Another life is mine in life and in death
    to make me courageous in the face of death or
    worse.

DISCOVERING THE THEOLOGY OF THE CROSS

The premise of this chapter and indeed of this whole book is that pastoral care consists not in removing someone's suffering but in helping the sufferer learn to interpret his or her sufferings in the light of the cross. Apart from the cross, the sufferer experiences a meaningless and out-of-control world that offers no hope. Such hopelessness makes suffering people vulnerable to our world's desperate invitations to take matters into their own hands and, if all else

24

fails, to eliminate suffering by eliminating the sufferer. This elimination of suffering people can be accomplished through neglect, abandonment, or even suicide and euthanasia. Anything to relieve the pain.

Although pastoral care is more a matter of helping people learn to interpret suffering than doing something to remove it, there are things pastors should *do* in order to help people live with their suffering—things such as baptizing, providing Holy Communion, praying, and reading Scripture. But even these pastoral doings presuppose the context of the cross of Christ. It is therefore the task of pastoral care to help the sufferer interpret all such "doings" in terms of the cross in the midst of a parishioner's suffering. Luther said, "He deserves to be called a theologian who comprehends the visible and manifest things of God seen through suffering and the cross."[1] And pastors are first and foremost theologians, called to shed light on the darkness of suffering lives. We are, as pastors, stewards of the mysteries of God, whether we want to be or not.

For many the extent of the significance of the cross means that we are saved from our sins by Christ's sacrificial death on the cross. We classically call this act of God our "justification." But "being saved" is not only a matter of fire insurance against hell or hope for the hereafter. Justification also means that we are reborn as new people, placed into the community of faith in order to live a new life here on earth. Living this new life in Christ is classically called our "sanctification." Both justification and sanctification find their center in the cross. Pastoral care consists in helping suffering people learn to relate the cross to their suffering here and now as well as to their hope for hereafter. Mr. Witti is such an example of personal suffering and the cross.

Theology of the Cross and Theology of Glory

Mr. Witti had asked for a visit from the hospital chaplain before surgery. Arriving at his room, I found him sitting in the chair beside his bed, trembling at the thought of cardiac bypass surgery the next morning. Hardened, not by temperament but by manual labor, he said little but asked me to pray with him. We prayed that all would go smoothly.

25

That was nearly two months ago, and Mr. Witti is still a patient in our intensive care unit. He is alert, but he is respirator dependent and requires kidney dialysis several times a week. Seemingly, our prayer for a smooth recovery without complications had gone awry.

What is remarkable about Mr. Witti, however, is his simple yet enduring faith in God. Although he has not been able to speak for nearly two months because of the respirator, he asks me each day (through hand signals) to pray with him. I do. We daily ask for faith to entrust to God all that comes that day. We also pray for the will of God to be done.

Each time we pray, Mr. Witti struggles to raise his hand to make the sign of the cross on his head and heart. This sign of the cross is no perfunctory ritual for Mr. Witti; he knows it is the cross that lies at the heart of one's confidence in the Lord.

Mr. Witti has a daughter. As we frequently stand together at the bedside, I often feel weary, frustrated, and empathetic toward Mr. Witti's sufferings; but his daughter is all smiles and lighthearted, reassuring her father that all will be well and that God will heal him. "There is nothing to worry about," she says. But somehow her father doesn't seem comforted by this and turns to me to make the sign of the cross. Unlike her father, Mr. Witti's daughter subscribes to a common misunderstanding of faith. She believes that her father will be healed, and she believes that faith is the way to health. There is no place for weakness and suffering in her understanding of the will of God. But Mr. Witti has surrendered to the will of God in confidence that God is still on his side. Mr. Witti's daughter, meanwhile, is still trying to get God to surrender to her will for her father.

The difference between Mr. Witti's and his daughter's understanding of God's ways illustrates the difference between what Martin Luther called the "theology of the cross" and the "theology of glory."[2] Luther coined these terms to express the distinction that St. Paul and the entire Scriptures make between God's ways and man's ways. Although the theology of the cross is difficult to grasp because of its sheer foreignness (it goes against every human instinct) and "foolishness,"[3] it is necessary to understand it in order to provide faithful pastoral care for sick, suffering, and dying people.

Luther says, "Without the theology of the cross man misuses the best in the worst manner,"[4] because the theology of the cross is the only way God works. "God wished to be recognized," not in health, wealth, and success, but "in suffering."[5] As much as parishioners may want to see the hand of God in nature's beautiful sunrises, moving stories of conversions, or success in parish programs, it is in the cross of Christ and in bearing their own crosses that God chooses to reveal his heart to them.

In speaking of the theology of glory Luther says, "A theology of glory calls evil good and good evil. A theology of the cross calls the things what it actually is."[6] Mr. Witti's daughter could not "call the thing what it actually is." She could not call the direction of her father's illness "death."

The disciples had the same problem with Jesus' words foretelling the cross. We are told that they didn't understand him, but I think they understood all too well. Theirs was a problem of denial and rejection. They didn't want it that way. Mr. Witti's daughter didn't want things to go the way of death, so she called evil good and held to a theology of glory.

In short, the theology of the cross says that God comes to us through weakness and suffering, on the cross and in our own sufferings. The theology of the cross says, "My grace is sufficient for you, for my power is made perfect in weakness."[7] The theology of glory on the other hand says that God is to be found, not in weakness but in power and strength, and therefore we should look for him in signs of health, success, and outward victory over life's ills. Mr. Witti could see God in his own sufferings; his daughter could not and, therefore, she looked for God in the healing she wanted to come from her faith and prayers. All of us hold to a theology of glory at times, not wanting to surrender all to God, but holding out for how we want God to appear and do his magic in the midst of our troubles.

If we do not understand the distinction between the theology of the cross and theology of glory, we will find ourselves drifting toward a theology of glory, in which our culture believes God works through the self-affirmation of pop psychology and instant gratification. We will begin to demand that God justify himself to us in our sufferings by giving us healing and success. We will demand a God who does what we want him to do, and we will reject the way of the cross by which he comes to us. We will become fearful of suffering and preoccupied with its avoidance at the expense of truth and faithfulness, calling the evil of euthanasia "good" and the good of suffering "evil."

Tragedy and Comedy Under the Cross

Gene Edward Veith illustrates the theology of the cross and the theology of glory in another way. In describing a "tragic sense of life and the comic sense of life,"[8] he uses Dante's definition of tragic and comic in literature. Dante says, "A tragedy is a story that begins in joy but ends in pain. A comedy is a story that begins in pain but ends in joy." Veith poses the question for us, "Is life ultimately tragic or comic? Those with a comic sense of life expect suffering now ... those with a tragic sense of life do not expect suffering now. ... The Christian world-view encourages a comic sense of life."[9]

If a person holds to a tragic view of life that pursues happiness now at any cost, a view that devalues the sufferings of this life, he will inevitably hold to a theology of glory, seeking to avoid suffering—perhaps even to the point of despair and self-destruction in suicide. If he holds to a comic view of life that accepts the inevitability of suffering now and anticipates the joy in the end, he will hold to a theology of the cross that enables him to see God's strength in the weakness of his sufferings. This person will find peace in entrusting his weakness to God's strength. He may even learn to laugh at the futility of taking his own suffering and pain too seriously. Veith reminds us that "what we are laughing at in comedies is human pride running smack up against human limits."[10]

Living in a culture that doesn't believe there are any limits to human accomplishment, we could easily carry into the Christian life a sense of utilitarianism which believes that only the lack of method and not human sin prevents us from conquering all. On our old hospital library wall hangs a dedication that ends, " ... with the hope that study and contemplation within its walls will help you relieve suffering and put away death." Quite a goal and expectation for human accomplishment! Some in the church also believe that "when the going gets tough, the tough get going." This theology of glory leads to a 10-step type of approach to solving sin's dilemmas. Solution, it would appear, depends on method rather than on grace.

Some might wish that this book had been titled *Ten Steps toward Better Living with Suffering,* a list of things for us to do in order to avoid or relieve suffering and replace it with prosperity of body, mind and heart; but that is not the way of the cross. That way is the human way of the theology of glory. Conversely, by way of the cross, God speaks to us through suffering. The way of the cross is "foolishness to those who are perishing" and wisdom to those who are being saved. It is not that we are in a sadistic search for misery or that we enjoy suffering; it is simply that we do not believe that the ultimate elimination of suffering in this life comes by means of human accomplishment, not even if it's done in the name of God. Rather than the human spirit against the world, the flesh, and the devil, we follow a God who leads us to the foot of the cross for relief. It is there we look for direction.

FROM "WHY" TO "WHERE"

If pastoral care consists not in doing something to remove suffering but in interpreting suffering in the light of the cross, then we must begin with what God chooses to reveal, not with what people want God to reveal. Today people feel little need to justify themselves before God, but rather demand that God justify himself to us. Therefore, the most common question they will raise in the face of suffering is, "Why is God doing this to me?" And although there may be a trace of genuine search for God's will in suffering, more likely the question betrays an underlying attitude that means to say, "I don't deserve this; God should treat me better than this."

Ultimately, the appropriate question is not "Why is God doing this?" but "Where is God in this?" Where is God in my suffering? The "why" of suffering, motivated by the demand that God justify himself to us, is a pointless question. Answers that say God is testing us, punishing us, teaching us, or warning us—such answers rarely fit the particulars of our or another's situation. Since we do not know the mind of God, we cannot know when or whether these answers fit at all. Job found that his question "Why are you doing this to me?"

got no answer other than a response that prefigured the cross. It is to the foot of the cross that pastors must lead their parishioners. There will be resistance to being led there. All demands of God for answers and all human pride that feels it deserves answers must end up as excess baggage at the foot of the cross. Rather than "why," better to ask "where." "Where is God in suffering? My suffering?" God answers with the reply, "Right in the middle of it!"

God in the Midst of Suffering

A theology of glory distances us from God and from one another. Some of the most difficult patients I have had to minister to in the hospital have been well-intentioned Christians who have refused to acknowledge their fears and concerns in the face of life-threatening illness.

Dawn, a cancer patient in her mid 30s, had not been a church-goer until her coming to faith in college days. There she not only found Christ, but a community of friends who shared that faith and were a constant presence in her life now in her illness. These devoted people prayed for her, not only in private but at her bed-side, keeping vigil with her in twos and threes daily. As is often the case for pastors wanting to be a support to parishioners, the constant presence of concerned people made it difficult to speak to Dawn alone about her fears and concerns. It was almost as if these devoted friends were there to protect her from doubt and the threatening prospect of facing these things.

Dawn and her friends were involved in a "conspiracy of faith," trying to hold off the devil and death itself with prayer and mutual encouragement. Unfortunately, Dawn and her friends believed that illness and death were enemies that could be controlled and defeated by their faith. This faith seemed to border at times on a "power of positive thinking." Together they stood against the Evil One and fought any attempt to expose Dawn's fears about her ill-ness or pending death. Their naivete toward the power of sin and death thrived on the theology of glory and kept Dawn isolated in the midst of friends. In fact, it kept the friends spiritually and emo-tionally isolated from each other, almost as if some code of ethics forbade them to talk about defeat and death. Faith and faithfulness were on the line, and the threat was overwhelming.

Toward the end, Dawn became depressed and withdrawn, no doubt due in part to her not being allowed to share deeper feelings. The vigil remained, but became subdued and shaky. No one seemed to know what to do in the face of impending death. When the day of Dawn's death came there was no "peace that passes all human understanding"; but there was an atmosphere of defeat, with no focus on Christ's victory in the midst of suffering. The theology of the glory had done its damage.

The theology of glory not only distances us from God but parishioners from pastors, and pastors from parishioners. There are many pastors who unknowingly create a distance from their parishioners in the name of God. They communicate the attitude, "If you have faith you can get through this; God never gives you more than you can bear!" Platitudes and slogans, usually in the form of Bible passages, characterize the pastoral visit. While there is truth in what these pastors say, their timing is off or their words don't fit the situation. More important, platitudes do not reflect sensitivity to the parishioner's particular needs at the moment. Cliches and slogans ought to be left to bumper stickers, not the bedside. We will explore better ways to visit the suffering later in this book. Meanwhile it should be noted that pastors sometimes unknowingly foster a theology of glory rather than enter the suffering of people at the foot of the cross.

THE BRIDGE BETWEEN GOD AND US

The theology of the cross bridges the distance between us and God, a gap created by the theology of glory. When a parishioner tries to be strong in the midst of suffering, believing this to be an act of faith, she may well be resisting God's self-revelation in the midst of weakness. When Dawn and her friends worked hard at supporting each other in the faith, they actually refused to acknowledge some of the fears and feelings they were experiencing on a deeper level. These fears and feelings were not (as they supposed) enemies to be resisted but part of the suffering through which God makes himself known to us as compassionate and forgiving. There is in each of us the desire to avoid death. While with Paul we might genuinely desire to "depart and be with Christ," on a deeper level we still desire to live because God has built that desire into us. From the beginning it was not God's desire for us to die, but to live on this earth. The life he gives each newborn is a life to be lived here and now. Christians ought never disparage this life no matter how painful or difficult it may be at times. Faith acknowledges the gift of life and the validity of living with hope even in a fallen world.

Fear of death, then, is natural and appropriate. We will expand on this thought in a later chapter, but for now it is enough to acknowledge our repugnance at the threat of death. Jesus found it to be the same. Our Lord's experience in the Garden of Gethsemane is a part of the theology of the cross. There we see Jesus, afraid to die and considering the avoidance of death. Jesus asks his heavenly Father to allow the whole thing to be taken away from him. It is only after Jesus begins by acknowledging his revulsion toward death and his fear of death's sting that he is ministered to by angels sent from the Father to comfort him. Prior to this, as he knelt in prayer, he experienced nothing but agony and bloody sweat.

If we are naive toward the presence of sin and its power to kill, we will attempt to overcome suffering by our own strength, sometimes calling our strength "faith." However, by whatever means we attempt to take on sin and death ourselves, we are following the theology of glory, not the theology of the cross. Only Jesus Christ can take on death and overcome it.

Our calling is to kneel at the foot of the cross and acknowledge our fears and helplessness. Entrusting all to him, we find hope through what he has done on that cross for us. This daily experience of being humbled at the foot of the cross in the midst of our suffering is the way of the cross, our sanctification. It is painful. Daily, the Old Adam is put to death, and we find ourselves dead to our own sins and resources—including the resource of faith, which we suppose is our contribution to God's ability to save in the midst of suffering.

Truly it is by grace that we are saved even in the midst of suffering. Martin Luther described our life in Christ as a daily death and resurrection in which the old sinful self is drowned and the new person in Christ is raised to life to face another day. The drowning takes place in our repentance and in our remembrance of who and whose we are through Baptism. The way of the cross is humbling, not exalting. Exaltation comes in the end.

Perhaps the most dominant characteristic of people who live under the theology of the cross is their acknowledgment of helplessness in the face of suffering. A culture that values self-determination and personal control over any outside authority or influence will not find the theology of the cross appealing. Even Christians are so much a part of the world in which they live that they frequently do not recognize the influence of values and norms at work in them against their faith.

Pointing to God

The goal of pastoral care under the cross is not to try to eliminate suffering but to point the parishioner to God in the midst of suffering. Others have as their task the elimination of suffering, up to a point. God calls doctors, nurses, therapists, technicians, and counselors to relieve suffering. Pastoral care, on the other hand, is concerned with the presence of God in the midst of suffering. It concerns itself with helping the suffering parishioner to see God there.

The posture of kneeling at the foot of the cross enables us to see God at work in suffering. Ironically, our helplessness makes it possible to see God. This is true not only for the suffering parishioner but also for the pastor who suffers with the suffering parishioner. Understanding this, we might say (carefully understood) that the experience of defeat and the feeling of helplessness is good for pastors. Jesus experienced apparent defeat and helplessness, and we called it *Good* Friday. Suffering puts us at the foot of the cross, beside parishioners, where together both sufferers discover the meaning of the cross and the peace that does "pass all human understanding." Defeat is the way of the cross, but ironically, defeat acknowledged in faith becomes victory.

The Pastor as Cross-Bearer

A Pastor's Prayer

In the cacophony of life,
    when the screams of the world,
        with the cries of busyness,
            tear at the world's soul,
    I hope for a voice of sanity!

When the emptiness of RELIGION,
    coupled with the certainty of
        pluralistic nothingness,
            demands to be heard,
    I hope for a voice of truth!

With the temptation to flaunt
    dogmatism and rejection,
        and the loudness of voices
            that do not listen,
    I hope for a voice of God!

Two Pastors

One of the first hospital calls I made after ordination was in response to a request from a parishioner to visit her elderly father. He had become suddenly ill and was in critical condition. He was a member of another parish 30 miles away, and his family had tried in vain to contact his pastor. The family had already gathered at his bedside in the small community hospital when I arrived at what turned out to be the hour before his death. The family did not know me, but allowed me to share this intimate moment with them. My parishioner, Adele, shed quiet tears and, standing beside me, grasped my arm tightly with both hands as if to hold

34

me there. Perhaps she sensed that as a young pastor, feeling inadequate, I would rather have been anywhere but there. Her father's breaths became increasingly shallow, and when the end came he seemed to fade away without our realizing it. Even after acknowledging his death, the family remained at the bedside, tearful but speaking comfortingly to each other. I wept with them, and I am sure my sense of helplessness said little more than that these people were not alone. "In the stead and by the command of my Lord Jesus Christ" I was there as God's way of being with them in their sorrow.

At this point the door burst open and in flew the deceased's pastor. He had finally gotten word of the situation. Bible in hand and overcoat flung over his arm, he rushed to the bedside and seemingly ordered the family to pray with him. In moments he was in and out.

There must have been some content to his words of comfort, and perhaps he did greet me (we knew each other), but it all happened so fast and the tone of his visit stood in such sharp contrast to the gentle death that had just occurred that, to this day, his visit is little more than a blur in my memory. I am certain that my own minimal involvement stunned me as much as this pastor's attempt at pastoral care, but I remember feeling angry at him even as it was happening. As I drove home from the hospital in the solitude of my car, I exploded bitterly at his insensitivity. I had felt helpless in the face of death, but this pastor seemed detached and insensitive. Still, he had done his thing, and I hadn't done much of anything; but each of us had made an attempt to help these grieving people carry the cross in suffering.

When Jesus invites a disciple to "deny himself and take up his cross and follow," he invites him to put away obsession with self and to be a faithful witness to Christ in the face of death. Jesus said, "Whoever wants to save his life will lose it, but whoever loses his life for me will find it" (Matt. 16:25). Every situation that poses a choice between witness to self and witness to Christ is a matter of bearing the cross, for it puts us at odds with the world's obsession with self. We are warned that in the end times "people will be lovers of themselves" (2 Tim. 3:2).

35

Concern for self and self-fulfillment has influenced bioethics to adopt the language of "rights." The language of rights concerns itself with procedural rather than substantive matters. That is, having lost objectivity as a society and having accepted relativism in values, our society is unable to say what it is that gives life meaning. In place of any absolute meanings, the focus is on the process of working toward "fulfillment"—without any hope of getting there. We will never arrive, according to this relativism, because there are no absolutes at which to arrive. So we are encouraged to value relative process, not absolute substance, as life's goal.

In contrast, the Christian's goal in life is not to engage in procedure wrapped in the language of individual rights. Rather, the Christian's goal grows out of the substantial conviction that we come from and are redeemed by God to live for and return to our Lord Jesus Christ. In this Christ we find fulfillment. Since the cross makes possible this substantive goal, it is in bearing the cross that we find fulfillment in life and in death. Pastors are called to bear their parishioner's crosses with them, and not to worry about self-fulfillment. William Hulme said it well nearly 30 years ago: "The antidote to the minister's despair is his involvement in the lives of his people."[1]

Pastors are cross-bearers with others who suffer. Whether we do it well or poorly, it is part of our calling. Making hospital calls, visiting nursing homes, encouraging the elderly, and supporting the helpless are part of the pastor's way of the cross. In the story told earlier, the second pastor attempted to take charge in the name of God. He chose to have little personal involvement in the lives of his parishioners, rather performing the duties of his calling as a functionary. Ironically, I later discovered that his parishioners thought no less of him for it. In fact, they saw him as God's presence to them as much as I had hoped I was.

My own helplessness in the face of death seemed a problem to me at the time, but feeling helpless never feels good. In this case, however, to take charge and do something as an attempt to erase or cover up the pain of this death seemed a worse thing. To take charge is to succumb to the temptation to espouse the theology of glory, whereas a willingness to feel helpless in the face of suffering may be called being faithful. It is, after all, in faithfulness to the suffering Christ of the cross that we are called to be pastors. Glory will have to wait for the Second Coming.

THE PASTOR'S PSYCHOLOGICAL MAKEUP

My story of two pastors illustrates not only differences in the pastoral care of parishioners and the difference between a theology of the cross and a theology of glory, but also differences in the psychological makeup of pastors. As much as pastors may be convinced that they are motivated by the Holy Spirit (and as Christians they are), they are also motivated by a complex maze of psychological factors. Without becoming saturated in a narcissistic approach to life, as is our culture, it is legitimate and helpful for pastors to understand themselves psychologically. Knowledge of our psychological makeup can help us understand our parishioners' struggles as well as our own difficulty in choosing the theology of the cross rather than a theology of glory. Twentieth-century psychology has made us sensitive to our feelings and the inner workings of the mind—a necessary starting point for what cultures of the past have called "wisdom." Psychology can also make us aware of obstacles that complicate relationships with people, characteristics in us that distance us from one another and that jeopardize wholesome intimacy. Pastors need to understand their own psychological makeup (as much as they are able) in order to practice appropriate intimacy with people who are suffering.

As useful as psychology is in helping us to look at our feelings and the inner workings of the mind, we must always understand psychology within the context of a fallen world. There is a difference, for example, between the aim of Christian introspection and the aim of narcissistic introspection.

Christians look inwardly, with the aim of repentance over what they may find there; whereas pop psychology invites us to look inwardly only to indulge and accept whatever is found there. Such authentic indulgence is valued more by our culture than the confession of authentic sins. Nevertheless, faced with the best and worst of psychology, pastors must learn to examine their own psychological makeup while at the same time rejecting the trivialization of self-fulfillment in favor of the fulfillment that comes in serving others. Better ministering to others compels the pastor to pay attention to his own psychological makeup.

This story of two pastors also demonstrates what the Christian psychiatrist Paul Tournier called "the strong and the weak" response to a crisis. Tournier does not place a moral value on "strong or weak," as if strong were better than weak; but he simply wants us to understand that each of us is psychologically motivated as well as spiritually motivated. For example, if called to do so, each of us pastors might have attempted to justify our pastoral care of this family either on the basis of the family's need for a compassionate presence or a demonstration of pastoral authority.

However, I suspect that neither of us was much aware of our own psychological workings at the moment when we were each called upon to help the grieving family. I responded in what Tournier would call a "weak" way, whereas the patient's pastor responded in what he would call a "strong" way. By "weak" Tournier means inhibition, including the possibility of "depression and sadness, and withdrawal into one's shell and silence."[2] The other pastor responded with a "strong" reaction, by which Tournier means excitation, "sometimes exhilaration and condescension, rashness and aggressiveness, even glibness."[3] Tournier adds, "strong reactions lead to conflicts only indirectly, in so far as resistance is encountered,"[4] which may explain why I was angry with this pastor's pastoral care but the family was not.

At that time I was uncomfortable with my "weak" expression of pastoral care of this family. Although there are many times when I feel skilled in pastoral care, there are still times when I feel helpless in the face of sickness and death. However, I am not as uncomfortable with my weakness as I used to be. Discovery of the theology of the cross has helped put it into perspective. It is human to want to avoid feeling helpless and out of control, though there are always humbling times when such feelings are appropriate. They remind us that, although we may be helpless, God is not.

I remember being called into the hospital in the middle of the night by a nurse who was going to disconnect a patient's pacemaker at the request of the family. The family had asked a chaplain to be present for this event. On the way to the hospital, I writhed in the revulsion I had for this sort of thing and wondered what I would say that might cause the family to think more carefully about their actions. I felt totally helpless. Even as I entered the Intensive Care Unit, nothing came to mind. Walking up to the bedside to greet the family, I learned from the nurse that they hadn't waited for my arrival but had turned off the pacemaker, only to have the patient's heart begin to function normally again without it. The family looked at me as if to say, "Now what do we do; he didn't die?" Without thinking, I said, "Perhaps the Lord is just reminding us who is in charge." The family nodded in agreement and our conversation turned to the care of the patient under the providence of God. In the face of my helplessness, God had taken charge of the situation, letting me in on the final act. God's power through weakness!

Other psychological needs also motivate pastors more than they may realize. The need to be loved or at least liked motivates most of us at least as much as the desire to love others. When we feel unloved or not liked by someone, we may react by withdrawing from and rejecting that person or by aggressively holding to our point of view or course of action. Aggressiveness is usually motivated by a certain amount of hidden anger or even by deeper rage; but the pastor may not see this in himself, believing that spiritual intentions are prompting his rash actions. When the parishioner then responds negatively to the pastor's aggressiveness, the pastor may feel confused, unappreciated, and unloved—and react by feeling hurt, claiming that he "only meant the best" for this parishioner. Feeling hurt is one of many learned responses we develop early in life as a way of coping with the disapproval of others. It can be a way of gaining sympathy from others and of protecting ourselves from what we perceive to be angry people. No one, we believe, will hit a man when he is down. In feeling hurt, we make the erroneous assumption that we are being misunderstood and we don't have to admit that our own actions or attitudes have contributed to the parishioner's becoming angry with us. So, if the family had become angry with the second pastor for his rash entry and abrupt departure, the pastor may have "chosen" (it is not a conscious choosing) to feel hurt and withdraw from the family until they learn, in his mind, to appreciate him more. Or possibly, the pastor might write an angry letter to the family saying that he only meant the best when he "barged in." Pastors sometimes find it difficult to admit that their motives may not be as spiritually noble as they had thought.

Another example of psychological influence centers on one of the most common complaints of pastors: the feeling of being trapped in ministry. Not only may the pastor not have an opportunity to leave his present church and find another, but he may feel trapped by routine or by parishioners' resistance to change. The pastor's knowledge of his own psychological makeup hopefully will expand as he grows older and experiences more successes and failures with people. For example, the pastor who is bored with his ministry feels trapped, thinking he needs a change when he may not be bored at all. What he calls boredom (restlessness) may be anxiety over some subtle or overt conflict in the parish or in his family life. If a pastor feels bored with his ministry and if he understands boredom as not having enough to keep him busy, possibly he has lost his creative edge, is depressed, or is uncertain and anxious about how to deal with his frustrations. Rather than taking flight and running up against the same thing in himself in another parish, it is important for him to learn to recognize his pattern of facing his anxieties and deal with them before moving on.

There is no sin in the pastor's being frustrated, angry, or anxious. However, when he calls these feelings something other than what they are, they can quickly lead him in the direction of sin. "The theology of the cross calls a thing what it is."[5] Of course, some pastors are aggressive toward people, not because they are angry but simply because they are inept and unskilled in pastoral care. Like the apostle Paul, they also can learn that God's "power is made perfect in weakness." The redeeming feature of pastoral ministry is that God can work even through our ineptness or anger. This too is the theology of the cross.

Modeling Pastoral Care

The pastor needs to pay attention to his psychological needs both for his own integrity and also to be a role model to his parishioners. The task of modeling pastoral care for parishioners is part of the challenge of pastoral ministry. His modeling is a way of teaching his parishioners how to care for others. Such modeling is, of course, humanly flawed, but the pastor's life is characterized by grace and faithfulness nevertheless. The first thing a pastor has to learn in being a cross bearer is to bear it in weakness and not feel he has to be in control of the situation.

Modeling pastoral care begins in the pastor's home. The attention a pastor gives to the spiritual, emotional, and psychological needs of his family is crucial. "He must manage his own family well and see that his children obey him with proper respect. (If anyone does not know how to manage his own family, how can he take care of God's church?)"[6] Today pastoral families are disintegrating almost as quickly as other families. A survey recently revealed that pastors' wives believe that their highest need is for a female friend with whom they can freely share their frustrations as pastors' wives. The pastor's ministry begins at home, where he learns to listen to his wife's needs, where he learns to understand his teenager's problems, and where he confesses his own sins and receives the forgiveness of his family in the name of God.

Shortly after Sue and I were married, following our first argument, I admitted my fault and she admitted hers. What was difficult for me was not confessing my sin but hearing my wife say "I forgive you." Her absolution confirmed my confession. Until then, I had glibly said "I'm sorry" without thinking of it as a confession of *sins*.

Over the years we have pronounced absolution on each other often, and it has always given us a fresh starting place in our relationship. Our children also learned that it is a relief to admit wrongs, receive forgiveness, and get on with life again in a better way with each other. For us, starting over following confession and absolution meant going back to the disagreement and learning to listen to each other in order to find a good solution for our problem.

It is always "our" problem rather than "your" problem. If any person in a marriage or family thinks there is a problem, then there is a problem, even if it is not personally a problem for the other. Learning this at home can help pastors acknowledge the needs and concerns of others for the sake of the whole body of Christ, the church. Of course, some things don't deserve the same amount of attention as others, either in the parish or at home. In any case, it is vital that the pastor's attention to his own family be the starting place for his ministry.

It is important for the pastor to set the priorities: wife first, children next, then parishioners. When emergencies or other circumstances rotate this order of priorities, it is important to return to it as quickly as possible. Except for those parishioners who have unresolved conflicts in their own families, most parishioners will appreciate this modeling, because it also encourages them to establish these same priorities (of which they may have lost sight, even though they know the sequence is right). Jesus spent quality time with his inner circle of disciples to prepare them to bear witness to Christ in his absence. The pastor's family becomes the inner circle that provides him with an intimacy necessary to minister, in an appropriate way, to others.

In summary, the pastor must accomplish several tasks in learning to be a cross-bearer. First, he must learn to accept his own limitations and weaknesses before he supports others in bearing theirs. This begins with the theology of the cross, the Good News that God works through weakness. When the pastor carries his cross, admitting weakness and sins, entrusting himself to God, others will learn to do the same.

Second, to be a cross-bearer, the pastor must give attention to his growth in faith and to his psychological growth. As he becomes more aware of his strengths and weaknesses and gains insight into his own motives, he will realize more than ever that God works through him by grace. What a relief to learn this! God calls him, not to be successful in what he does but to be faithful, regardless of results. Much of pastoral care is a matter of waiting to be surprised by the work of the Holy Spirit. This too is the theology of the cross.

3

Suffering, Sickness, and the Cross

It Is as If!

It is as if I have never been sad
    or pained or without hope or lacking in joy.
It is as if the world had been good
    and the evil one caged.
It is as if death never came
    and sickness and age lacked all substance.
It is as if fright and rage
    and loneliness and dullness never existed.
It is as if life goes on and on
    in expectation of the Coming One
        who was, and is, and is to come.

THE INEVITABILITY OF SUFFERING

There is in our culture an underlying belief that if researchers only had enough money, a cure for every disease could eventually be found. We place our hopes for such cure in the hands of laboratory scientists, medical doctors, and pioneers in new technology. But Christians also know that we live in a fallen and imperfect world. We know that there will always be suffering due to physical and mental illness. Although we want to believe in the possibility of a cure for every disease, we also accept the reality that this is a sinful world. None of us will get out of it alive, for "the wages of sin is death."

There will always be pain and suffering in the world. Yet for our purpose of understanding pastoral care, we distinguish between pain and suffering. While most illness causes some pain, not every-

43

one who experiences pain is necessarily suffering. Pain can be defined as a greater or lesser degree of physical discomfort. For example, pain usually follows surgery, and pain medication is given for relief. Suffering, on the other hand, can be defined as the existential anxiety, fear, worry, or hopelessness that may or may not accompany pain. Suffering is a reaction to pain.

Some years ago I visited Jack in the hospital after he broke his leg in a fall at work. He required surgery and a lengthy course of physical therapy. Shortly into therapy it became evident that Jack did not want to overcome his pain and, in fact, needed his pain as an excuse to avoid therapy. Physical therapy would have enabled him to return to a job he hated. Actually, Jack had hoped for a permanent disability due to his accident as a way to free him from his job. Not Jack's pain but the possibility of losing his pain caused Jack's suffering. Pastoral care addressed Jack's suffering, not his pain, and helped him face his anxiety. Jack found spiritual strength to work toward recovery and to return to work. Attention to suffering is the operating theater of pastoral care.

It is ironic that at a time in history when pain control is more available than ever before, there also seems to be less ability to manage the suffering that remains. Patients I have visited in recent years seem less equipped to face suffering than they did even 20 years ago. The medical profession's interest in pain clinics is one response to the realization that physical pain is not always the cause of suffering. Obviously, opportunity to provide spiritual care to those who are suffering is greater than ever, and for pastors it can be an important aspect of pastoral care.

Pastoral care is concerned with the interpretation of suffering, a process in which a parishioner is helped to see God in the midst of it all. Such a holy perspective reveals that God is involved in suffering in order to deepen faith and provide hope. If a pastor tries to relieve a parishioner's anxiety without helping him look at his suffering, the parishioner may be denied an opportunity for spiritual growth. Merely to aim at removing suffering may be to succumb to the theology of glory. The theology of the cross helps a parishioner wrestle with his relationship to God in suffering. The fact that God chooses mysteriously to come to us in the person of

44

his Son, Jesus Christ, in the midst of his suffering on a cross, is significant. Learning to carry our crosses faithfully is also significant.

In the Garden of Gethsemane Jesus both begins his journey to the cross and shows us how to bear our cross in our suffering. Jesus rejects the escape route available to him because he is God, which might make it possible to avoid suffering. He struggles, as all struggle, with the weight of sin (although not his own) and with the grief it produces. What we see of Jesus in Gethsemane is significant, not only for our redemption but also for our learning to suffer faithfully. Here Jesus' physical symptoms express spiritual realities; the physical agonies are the product of his "grief." We can begin to understand Jesus' grieving as resulting from his anticipation of death as the wages of sin. He becomes physically ill, sweating bloodlike drops of sweat, showing signs of anxiety and depression. It would miss the significance of the cross to dwell on the psychological or physiological aspects of this event, but the point here is simply to call attention to the connection between the physical and spiritual, between sin and suffering. When Jesus submits himself to God the Father and, thus, to suffering, God sends angels to comfort him. The Father does not remove Jesus' suffering. The cross still lies ahead, but Jesus is able to face suffering faithfully for us. In this experience of the physical and spiritual distress of Gethsemane and the process of Jesus' entrusting his suffering to his Father, we begin to see what it means to learn to live with suffering.

People have lived with suffering differently at different times. Until modern times the question asked by Christians was not "Why am I suffering" but "What shall my response be to God in the midst of it?" Western civilization in the 18th century gave birth to the rise of science, making a distinction between physical and spiritual. For the first time in history scholars believed that only the material world was real and that the spiritual was mere superstition. Consequently, attention shifted from the needs of body and soul to the needs of the body alone. The medical profession addressed pain, but neglected to help people deal with suffering. Attention to the suffering patient was divided between medicine and religion with an ever widening chasm separating them from one another.

Whereas the church of the Middle Ages lead its culture, providing spiritual meaning and support for suffering in illness, the church of today more often follows our culture, which bases its support on a physical and psychological model rather than on a spiritual one.

If the church through its pastors is to teach the world the connection between the sin and suffering, it must begin with the connection between sin and grace acted out on the cross. Paul illustrates these connections clearly in his attempt at pastoral care of the Christians in Corinth, when he points out that Christians can't expect to celebrate the Lord's Supper as if it were only a physical experience of eating and not a spiritual one as well. Because they erroneously considered only the physical aspects, Paul says, "Many of you are weak and ill, and some have died." "Let a man examine himself," Paul writes,[1] so that a person is aware of the reality of what is taking place in the Lord's Supper and what his participation means. Something more than eating and drinking bread and wine is going on here; the physical and the spiritual have blended.

This sacred understanding of the unity of the physical and the spiritual is the message that the world needs to hear, for the world is fragmented and suffering without meaning and without a community in which to discover that meaning. The church's practice of pastoral care speaks of the connection between sickness and sin as "cause and effect" (in the generic sense in which all sickness is part of living in a fallen world), it takes an important step in reuniting the physical and the spiritual. Seldom can sickness be traced back to a specific sin in an individual's life, and, if there is one, the pastoral counselor is advised to support the parishioner's voluntary discovery of this sin for himself rather than pointing it out to him. The story of Job's comforters cautions us not to presuppose specific sin as the cause of a person's suffering in a fallen world.

THEODICY AND THE THEOLOGY OF THE CROSS

Theodicy is the attempt to justify the ways of God to a suffering world. Harold Kushner popularized theodicy in our time in his best seller *Why Bad Things Happen To Good People.*[2] He suggests that there are only two answers possible: Either God can't prevent suffering, in which case we ought not be hard on God since he is doing the best he can; or God is cruel and enjoys making us suffer.

Kushner, attempting to defend God, of course favors the former and gets God off the hook by claiming that God is less than almighty. Somehow this is intended to comfort suffering people.

While theodicy attempts to justify the ways of God to a suffering person, what a person really needs in order to face suffering rightly is to stand justified before God. Stanley Hauerwas of Duke University rightly puts the focus of pastoral care back on the suffering parishioner rather than on attempts to justify the ways of God. He says, "We are . . . not interested in the theoretical issue of suffering and evil; rather, we are torn apart by what is happening to real people, to those we know and love."[3]

Christian attempts at theodicy are commonplace. For example, to say to a suffering person "God is just testing you to see if you will remain faithful" tries to justify God's ways or at least to explain them. This interpretation is sometimes followed by the promise of reward if we meet the test. Or, it is sometimes said, "God is punishing you for what you have done." This interpretation, although most frequently rejected on the surface, is the one that hits suffering people hardest at a deeper level, because they know they could have lived a better life and that they stand under the judgement of God in this life. Sometimes Christian theodicy explains suffering by saying that God is trying to "teach you something" or is "disciplining you."

Most insidious is this interpretation: "God has a plan for you and this is part of it." One must question a fatalistic outlook that sees God's "plan" as a static blueprint, oblivious to the moment-to-moment dynamic interaction of the person with God. It might be better to speak of God's plan for an individual as being "in the works"; that this plan is being worked out in God's mind daily along the way, as God listens and takes into account the responses of our lives and actions. Ultimately, the only plan of God we can be sure about is the plan for our salvation.

But none of these efforts at theodicy provides pastoral care to suffering people. For one thing, a pastor is presumptuous to claim to know the mind of God for any person. In fact, interpretation of suffering is better made by the sufferer than by another person, and retrospectively rather than prospectively. In the midst of suffering it is not always clear what purpose suffering serves. Perhaps

God keeps us off balance at the time to focus our attention on faithfulness rather than on explanations of suffering, asking us to pay attention to our suffering as the theology of the cross in action. The aim of pastoral care is to support the suffering parishioner in wrestling with God in this crisis of faith that holds potential for a deepening of that faith.

The theology of the cross speaks pastorally to suffering in a way that theodicy cannot. Sometimes, the sufferer will speak it to us. Vera was a woman in her late 60s whose daughter asked me to visit Vera in the hospital. Vera had had surgery for a brain tumor the previous day. As I entered her room, she was lying on her side in a fetal position, head bandaged, apparently sleeping. Standing by her bedside, observing the circumstances, I was surprised when she suddenly opened her eyes. She recognized me by my clerical collar, and I introduced myself as the hospital chaplain. She responded with a slight movement of the lips in an attempt to speak. I could not hear her and bent down to her. Still unable to hear, I pulled up a chair and came within inches of her lips. In a faint voice she whispered, "God has been so good to me!" Although hearing the words clearly, I was not sure I was hearing correctly. This damaged woman, unable to speak loud enough to ask the nurse for water, unable to foresee a future to her earthly life, was making a confession of faith in telling me that in the midst of all of this, God had been good to her. I was overwhelmed. These were the words I was supposed to say to her, but she taught me again the theology of the cross: God makes himself known in the midst and mystery of suffering.

THE MYSTERY OF SUFFERING

The cross, like suffering itself, is a mystery. Why God chose to make himself known in the midst of suffering on a cross, God only knows. Perhaps, if speculation is allowed, it is because it is there that we need him most. Or perhaps it is there that we least expect to see God, yet God does come—on his own terms, by grace. He cannot be cornered by our logic or theology. God is God and, as Bonhoeffer says, it is in learning to love God for God's own sake and not for what we can get from him or do with him that the Christian life is rightly lived.[4]

People have long attempted to clarify the mystery of illness. Some years ago, the Holistic Health movement provided an interesting and much needed picture of one aspect of the mystery of illness:

> Often when people are upset, or don't find much meaning, or damage a relationship, or are going too fast, or have lost something important, pretty soon they get so they don't feel so good anymore, and they get sick. So they go to the doctor, who looks at them, and fixes them, and gets them back on their feet. And then, because they haven't learned why they got sick, some people go home and they get upset again, and damage a relationship, and still don't find much meaning and go too fast again, or lose something important again. And in not too long, they get so they don't feel so good anymore and they get sick again. It's kind of wasteful and painful, but sometimes people go on like this: getting up and down forever. That is, until one time when they get sick and can't get gotten up again. We need physicians to help sick people up again by treating their sickness. We also need pastoral care people to keep them up by helping them deal with being upset, not finding meaning, going too fast, grief over losses, damage relationships, in their life.[5]

To discover meaning in illness, a parishioner needs to explore both his relationship with God and also his relationship with those with whom he lives. Generally, however, a person's first concern in illness is not for God or for other people but for oneself. Such an initial response will not hinder the discovery of meaning in illness if eventually the sick person shifts his focus back to God and to other people, because God comes through other people (ultimately through Jesus Christ). If there is brokenness in his relationship with God, that brokenness will flow over into his relationship with others, destroying needed intimacy. If there is brokenness in the relationship with spouse, for example, that brokenness will flow over into relationship with God. Pastoral care can provide the supportive environment needed for engagement with God and with people, allowing healing, reconciliation, and spiritual growth to take place. Most of all, pastoral care encourages a sick or suffering person to engage in a life-and-death struggle with God, an inevitable, hand-to-hand combat with God over "being upset, not finding meaning, going too fast, grief over losses, and damaged relationships." Furthermore, pastoral care urges the parishioner into this struggle in order to lose it (Luke 17:33) so that Christ can raise him up to new life.

HOSPITALS AS THE COMBAT ZONE FOR PASTORAL CARE

When I arrived as hospital chaplain at my present post, a priest in the community made it clear that he had no intention of visiting his sick parishioners and I wasn't to call upon him to do so. It wasn't that he didn't see the importance of visitation; he was just terrified of hospitals. It can be assumed that occasionally both pastors and parishioners will avoid hospitals and hospitalization for many reasons. When I was a hospital patient during my seminary years, one of my roommates visited me in order to offer support. He fainted during the visit! Some pastors may fear hospitals due to early childhood experiences. I remember counseling a man who, when he was six years old, was told by his parents that he was being taken to a birthday party when, in fact, he was being taken to the hospital to have his tonsils removed. My counselee recalls being dragged out, kicking and screaming, from under the hospital bed where he had taken refuge.

Hospitals can be frightening places. They require the suspension of personal safety, modesty, and independence. For many, hospitals are associated with dying even though, in our hospital for example, less than one percent of the nearly 400 patients die on a given day.

Hospitalization also requires a patient's dependency, not a popular concept in our present culture. For some, the experience of enforced dependency in childhood or observation of it in parental marriages has created connotations of oppression and abuse. In the past, unnecessary forced dependency may have existed in hospitals, and patients may have been treated with some condescension and/or paternalism by both physicians and nurses. Whether required or not, the fear of helplessness, the fear of loss of control, is the main reason many parishioners fear hospitals. They can no longer support the myth that they are in control of their lives and will never die.

People in our culture are losing not only the ability to live with suffering but also the ability to die gracefully in the face of what many are calling the indignities of treatment and medical care. Again, the issue is not the so-called indignity of the technology to which illness subjects us but rather the state of helplessness and loss of control that is related to sickness. Sickness reminds us of the brittle nature of what we call our autonomy. Hospitals and nursing homes are places where autonomy is dismantled and where dependency on God through the theology of the cross is enacted. It is the sinfulness of human nature to resist the cross and to grasp at a life where illnesses disappear and suffering will never have to be faced head on, where our myth of power and immortality continues undisturbed. Nevertheless, it is in the forced dependency of sickness and hospitalization that people are sometimes "dragged kicking and screaming into the Kingdom of God,"[6] as C. S. Lewis put it. To paraphrase a metaphor, it is easier for a surgeon to crawl through the eye of his needle than for a sick man to accept the theology of the cross.

51

4

Faith, Healing, and the Cross

Faith

Faith is to be able to doubt
as well as to believe.
Faith is to be troubled and hurting
as well as to be comforted ...
To be undergirded by God
is to be held together by Him
even as our world seems
to be falling apart!

THE CONNECTION
BETWEEN FAITH AND HEALING

In a culture that values a scientific understanding of disease and its treatment, the connection between the physical and spiritual aspects of illness is a somewhat unwelcome mystery. Nevertheless, the connection exists and lies at the heart of pastoral care of the sick and dying.

The case of Mildred points this out. Mildred had been a cancer patient for some months when I met her in our hospice unit. Alone, except for a sister, she was dying and knew it. Because Mildred suffered a growing depression, the nurse asked me to visit and to comfort her. Over a period of a few days Mildred and I became close enough for her to tell me her life's story. She had attended a Baptist church until the age of 12, when she moved to another state with her parents and never went to church again on a regular basis. Mildred continued to think of God, pray, and read her Bible. She attended various churches but never joined one. Now in her 70s,

52

she lay dying and regretted that she had never been baptized. She told me that she had always dreamed of being baptized in the Jordan River like Jesus. That now being an impossible dream, more than ever she felt alone and cut off from God and the community of faith, the church.

After instructing Mildred in the Christian faith and the meaning of Baptism, I asked her if she wanted to be baptized in the hospital before she died. She eagerly accepted. Arrangements were made with the physical therapy department to immerse Mildred in their pool, our approximation of the Jordan River. On the appointed day, her sister, some nurses, and several therapists gathered round the pool to witness as Mildred was lowered into the water and baptized.

What follows illustrates the mysterious relationship between faith and healing that medicine cannot explain. After her Baptism, Mildred's faith emerged and her depression disappeared. Over the next three weeks her physical condition improved dramatically. She was discharged from the hospital, her cancer arrested. Mildred returned to managing a downtown hotel where she had been employed.

About a year later, her cancer returned and Mildred was readmitted to the hospital, where she again was expected to die shortly. But Mildred was not the same person I had met a year earlier. She assured me that it had been a good year. "From the moment I was baptized, I never felt alone again. God has been with me, and I am part of the community of God's people on earth and, soon, in heaven." Within a few days Mildred died peacefully. Her faith had made her whole!

Faith is no stranger in the medical care of patients. A physician whose patient I had been visiting once wrote in the chart, "Patient cured by the chaplain." This physician no doubt enjoyed writing his comment as much for his own amusement as for his honest bewilderment at the effect of a pastoral visit. It also illustrates medicine's benign discomfort in acknowledging the place of faith in treating illness. Clergy frequently tell me that doctors do not take them seriously. Nonetheless, the pastor's presence at the bedside awakens a holy discomfort in doctors that is not likely to be dismissed. Pastors should value that discomfort and build on it constructively.

Faith against Medicine

What people in medical fields object to is the way some religious people pit faith against medicine. For example, an upbeat cleric with whom I served on a panel told an audience of nursing students that she had suffered much physical illness in the early years of her life, but after finding Jesus she no longer needed doctors or medicine. "I have Jesus," announced this faith healer, "and I have thrown all my medicine away." In the face of student skepticism, she did concede that before a sick person has Jesus, medicine might be necessary. Presumably, her expectation was that these student nurses were to help patients do away with medicine by making Christians of their patients.

The relationship between the physical and the spiritual and between faith and healing is not clear to us as a society or even to many in the church. Anyone visiting the hospitalized and offering to pray with patients no doubt sooner or later will run into the response, "Well, I guess it can't hurt." This minimalization of the relationship between faith and healing is as prevalent among the general population as among the medical profession. Living in this skeptical culture, many in the church also speak of two separate approaches to healing, the one by faith and the other by medicine, failing to appreciate the integration of faith and healing. In my visits with a woman with cancer of the cervix who had been rushed to the Intensive Care Unit following cardiac arrest, I pointed out to her physician that she had lost the will to live because her husband and children had recently died in a plane crash. The doctor responded, "That has nothing to do with her condition. She was just low on potassium." It would be a mistake to diminish the importance of potassium or to despise the magnificent technological side of medicine, but it is equally mistaken to divorce the spiritual from the physical. To see the connection between the spiritual and the physical, we look to the healing Jesus performed.

Why Jesus Healed the Sick

"I am the way and the truth and the life."[1] With these words of Jesus, we turn attention to healing in his ministry. It is especially significant that Jesus promises an eternity where sickness and sorrow no longer occupies our lives. Jesus' ministry was a foretaste of the life to come. In him we anticipate the promise, "Behold, the dwelling of God is with men. He will dwell with them, and they shall be his people, and God himself will be with them; he will wipe away every tear from their eyes, and death shall be no more, neither shall there be mourning nor crying nor pain any more, for the former things have passed away."[2] Jesus brought a new dimension to our understanding of healing when he healed illnesses before the end of time. The gospel of Luke takes up this theme in reporting the healings Jesus performed.

In Luke's first healing story[3] the demons ask, "Have you come to destroy us?" They know their days are numbered, but they are confused. They complain that the final curtain should not yet have fallen; Jesus is premature in his interference with sin and death. In the healings Jesus once performed, as in his suffering and dying on the cross, Jesus begins to bring to fulfillment the final words of Scripture, "Death shall be no more." As can be seen by these healings, a protective barrier is built to contain the ravages of sin and death; for those whom Jesus healed, limits are set beyond which sickness and death are not allowed to continue. Mildred experienced this with Jesus. In her experience of another year to live, there was a foretaste of things to come; it was a sign pointing to Jesus' victory even before the end and the Day of Judgement on the evil one.

Why Some Are Healed

Although it is ultimately presumptuous to ask God "Why am I not healed while others are," the question deserves consideration. The selective healing which does take place in this world is a gracious sign of things to come for all who have the eyes of faith to see it. In the midst of sickness and death God is reminding us that he is "for us" and not "against us," no matter how bad things may seem to be. God sprinkles gracious "drops of healing" from the heavens that fall on the just and the unjust alike. Some are touched and healed, others are not; but all who experience or witness the healing of one's many ills are given a hint of things to come in Christ. It is not that healing comes to some because they pray harder or are more faithful than others, but rather that God's grace anticipates again and again our need for a sign of the Kingdom among us.

Such healing takes place today in the most surprising ways and to the most unlikely people. A physician referred one of his patients to me saying with a wry smile, "If you convert him, I'll buy your lunch." The doctor then elaborated, "The patient is a college professor, a self-proclaimed atheist, a homosexual, an alcoholic, has end-stage liver disease, and is expected to die shortly." Taking the challenge more seriously than perhaps this physician expected, I called on the patient and introduced myself as the hospital chaplain. The patient made it immediately clear that he was an atheist and did not want to talk about God. Not easily put off I said, "Agreed! What would you like to talk about?" After a long pause he replied, "Well, why do *you* believe in God?" Our conversation lasted for nearly an hour. I closed by saying, "I know you don't believe in God, but I do, and I'd like to pray for you. Do you mind? You can just listen if you like." He agreed, and I prayed for his healing. When I finished praying, he said appreciatively, "That was nice; thank you." I acknowledged his appreciation and left.

In my next visit with him, as the hour drew to a close, he initiated the idea of prayer explaining, "Something happened when you prayed for me. After you left, I felt a peace that I have never felt before." After another three weeks this one-time-atheist and now-at-least theist was discharged from the hospital, his liver disease arrested. Although I never saw the man again, he assured me he had a friend who was a Christian and would talk with him further about God and the deeper healing which had begun in him. I never did collect my free lunch, but the patient's physician was both pleased and again mildly bewildered at his patient's recovery.

Healing and the Forgiveness of Sins

Unlike 20th-century thinking, Jesus allowed no separation between the physical and the spiritual in healing. The spiritual elite of his day were outraged, not because he blended the two, but because he connected the forgiveness of people's sins with the healing of their physical diseases. In the story of the paralyzed man brought by his friends for healing, Luke portrays Jesus not only as healer of physical sickness but also as healer of the sickness of the soul. Salvation is both physical and spiritual. We confess the same when we say, "I believe in the resurrection of the body" rather than the resurrection of only the soul.

The division, as we know it, between physical and spiritual did not occur until the 18th century. Until that time it was commonly understood that sickness and death were part of living in a sinful world. Physical realities had spiritual meanings, as Luke's story of the paralyzed man reveals.[4] Unable to do anything about his physical or spiritual needs, this paralyzed man is dependent on others to bring him to where he can find healing. Nowhere in Luke's gospel more than here do we find helplessness in illness and the importance of faithful people to address it. Friends who believe Jesus can help introduce this poor man to the healer, to Jesus. Surely, if the connection is to be made between physical and spiritual, it is people who believe in Jesus who will be the ones to help weak, helpless, and dying people make that connection.

Forgiveness and sickness are connected, but not in the way many might think. It is not that each illness is a punishment for a particular sin. This would be easier for some sick persons to accept than the Joblike frustration of searching the soul and finding nothing of great significance to confess. True, sometimes direct consequences result from our sinful behavior—AIDS from promiscuity, auto accidents due to drunken driving—but Jesus clearly denied that every illness is the consequence of particular or even accumulated sins. When asked by his disciples "Who sinned, this man or his parents," Jesus replied, "It was not that this man sinned, or his parents, but that the works of God might be made manifest in him."[5] Patients who perceive their sicknesses to be the result of particular sins ought to be listened to carefully, but pastoral caregivers ought not pursue this path with patients unless the connection is clear.

The connection between sickness, sin, and the need for forgiveness is ultimately deeper than particular sins. Jesus therefore points us to the cross for our care of sick, weak, and helpless people. The paralyzed man is a prime example. Unable to contribute anything, not even faith (it is the faith of his friends that impresses Jesus), he is nevertheless the recipient of forgiveness and healing from Jesus. The connection between sickness and the forgiveness of sins is the connection between our helplessness before God and the cross of Jesus on which Jesus became our help. But it is not that the cross merely gives us power to help ourselves or faith enough to be healed. Rather the cross is a sign that we are more diseased than we realize and that, in Jesus' victory over sin and death, we have been given something deeper than physical healing. This gift of God's grace to sick and dying people is the ultimate hope that sustains us through life, diseased as this world may be.

Faith, Healing, and the Cross

The theology of the cross must always be the lens through which we see the connection between faith and healing. It reminds us that God heals and that we do not—certainly not by our use of divine power given through faith. Faith is not power per se; rather, faith is trust in God, whether physical healing of our illness takes place in this life or not. Otherwise, we will be tempted to a theology of glory in which we merely use faith for our own ends, including the ends of "health and wealth" that become more important to us than God himself. If that seems unlikely, witness the attempts of some to convert people based on the promise of power from God to control life; promises that suggest that, if we only had enough faith, we could be healed or be rich or change the course of the world. Faith healers offer power first, God second. They tell us to believe in Jesus, not that we might love God for God's own sake, but that we might get from God what we want, namely healing or other benefits. The lust for more and more drives the appeal to believe in Jesus, assuming that only by believing will we get what we crave.

The theology of the cross keeps us honest. It reminds us, lest our illnesses preoccupy us, of the way things are in this sinful world. We will never get out of it alive. Therefore, we concern ourselves, not with the obsession of physical health and long life but with living faithfully, however long our lives. Faith is not a power tool that enables us to remake our lives, but an empty tool box that witnesses to our dependence on God as our Master Carpenter. The paralyzed man is healed, not because he had strength to believe in Jesus but because Jesus reached out to him in grace. His faith is not "power," but emptiness that trusts Jesus. Martin Luther put it well in his explanation of the Third Article of the Apostles' Creed: "I believe that I cannot by my own reason or strength believe in Jesus Christ, my Lord, or come to Him; but the Holy Spirit has called me by the Gospel, enlightened me with His gifts, sanctified and kept me in the true faith." Faith is always an open receptacle, not the power line to control a heavenly computer. The weakness of Jesus on the cross is the only "power" that is life to those who know they are dead without him.

BUT WHAT OF FAITH?

Faith does play a part in illness and healing for Christians. Faith asks whatever it desires, prays in hope for the will of God to be done in us, and receives what God gives. The will of God is not to be understood so much as a blueprint which we must somehow identify and follow as a pathway to success, but rather a dynamic and unrelenting intention of God for our welfare. Unlike the patient who, when all else fails, prays reluctantly and fatalistically "Thy will be done," the Christian recognizes God's will as a desired, confident, and joyful corrective of our bungling and frustrated efforts at determining what is best for us. To pray rightly "Thy will be done" is to trust that God's intentions toward us are good and gracious. To pray for the will of God might be to ask ultimately for the opposite of what we want and to trust that the unknown quantity of his intention is tempered by love for us. We ask for healing and we pray to live, but we do so with the overwhelming hope that the good and gracious will of God will override our request when necessary.

Prayer and Healing

How then shall we pray? Pray, not as a technique to get what we want from God but as a way of entrusting our lives to his care whatever that may encompass. Ministering to David helped me appreciate this difference. Nurses in the Intermediate Care Unit had asked me to support David, a 21 year old who had just arrived from the Intensive Care Unit. Battling the aftermath of a brain abscess, a complication of his having Lupus, David had become more aware of his own condition, and his fears and anxieties had escalated. When I first met this caring Baptist family, they warmly welcomed me. We spent a few visits sharing all David and his parents had been through with Lupus, since both David and his father had the disease.

David improved physically, and he was transferred from the Intermediate Unit to a general floor. His mental improvement allowed him to realize how close he had come to dying. Both David and his parents made maximum use of my visits to talk freely about their fears and God's dramatic deliverance in their lives. In the midst of their own weakness and helplessness they had come to see Jesus at their side through it all.

There was a day, however, when David seemed to fall apart emotionally. As I stepped off the elevator, I could hear a rattling of metal that increased in volume as I approached David's room. It was David's bed almost in motion. He was trembling with fear. Overwhelmed with all that he had been through, David's anxiety seemed to center on a spinal tap he was scheduled to undergo that afternoon. It was necessary to insert a needle between his vertebrae, draw off spinal fluid, and determine the possibility of residual infection from the brain abscess. He was terrified of what he believed would be the pain of such a procedure and announced it in clear metallic tones. Medication and the soothing assurances of the nursing staff had failed to calm him.

David and I talked above the rattling din, and I admitted that I could make no assurances that there would not be pain since I had never experienced this procedure personally. Nor was it my task to say so one way or the other. But I told him there was something we could do about the fear that was turning him into a basket case. In the closing minutes of our visit I told David what I wanted him to do. "David, when they come to do the test, I want you to close your eyes and picture Jesus, however you picture him, and I want you to say to him, 'Jesus, I can't handle this. I am afraid and I put my fear into your hands. You handle it for me.' " I reinforced the need for David to leave that fear in Jesus' hands and not take it back again. We prayed and I left.

Hours later I met David's parents in the hallway; they were smiling the widest grins I had ever seen them smile. "You'll never guess what happened," they said. "David did what you said and was so relaxed he fell asleep during the test." They urged me to go hear it from David himself, which I did immediately. This time as I entered the room, David greeted me with elation. Looking at the two nurses attending him, he said, "The nurses gave me medicine to calm me, but it didn't do anything. The doctors couldn't relax me. But this man of God told me to put my fears in Jesus' hands, and I did—and it worked!" David continued to announce to everyone who entered his room for the next week the wonderful works of God in his life. David was free of his fears and recovered rapidly. At 21 he was made an elder in his church and with his father gave witness to the newness of faith that had come to them.

Although I fear lest David's story reflect a "theology of glory," of the "power of faith to do great things," it would be a mistake to understand it that way. Nor should this "power" be bottled and marketed at Christian publishing houses as a spiritual technique for others to follow. True, God graciously responded to David's helplessness and emptiness, and God's power was made perfect in David's weakness. Yet David may have to suffer much in years to come. His experience of victory over terror can not assure him that he can control all things himself by pulling the right strings, even "faith strings." The theology of the cross reminds us that the grace David experienced always comes in spite of us rather than because of us. Our faith is the recipient of God's grace, not the wage earner of it. God's message to David is always, "My grace is sufficient for you," whether healing takes place or not. This is the real cause for a celebration such as David enjoyed following his mountaintop experience of faith. David had entrusted his life to God and was willing to bear whatever God gave in response to that trust.

Praying Rightly?

Some pastors hesitate to include a bedside prayer for healing, especially if death seems near. However, we are invited to pray against all odds of illness. I emphasize this with caution. A family or a patient should never assume that God will always delay death or remove illness. Nevertheless, cases I have illustrated in this book attest to God's control, even over death.

There have been times when I have prayed for death with patients. I have never done so lightly, but usually when the patient has asked me to do so. It is important to see prayer, not as taking charge of life or death but as a way of putting all things into the hands of God and finding peace in doing so. Prayer also prevents us from succumbing to fatalism that says "I guess my time just isn't up yet," as if there were an alarm clock in heaven with our nametag on it. Such a deterministic understanding does not allow for God's dynamic intervention in every moment of our life. God indeed has plans for us, but it is not a foregone conclusion how he will resolve things. Prayer is not a tool of faith by which we control his control over our lives. Rather it is the conversation God began with us when he established a relationship with us in Baptism. As his children we can ask anything.

THE AIM OF FAITH IN HEALING

The purpose of faith in the healing process is to help patients connect with God in a way that puts life into holy perspective. As sickness testifies to the fallenness of this world, so healing points to the kingdom of God that comes to the just and the unjust alike. Healing is a sign of hope for things greater than physical welfare. The possibility of healing is always present, along with the deeper healing of our relationship with God and with one another that God is bringing about in the grace he pours upon us in Christ Jesus. Pastors and other Christian givers of spiritual care need to value physical healing as a sign of spiritual healing.

Having come to a greater understanding of the theology of the cross in Part 1, we are ready now to move on. In Part 2, I will explore further the practicalities of such care under the cross.

PART 2

The Cross in Action: Practical Pastoral Care in Specific Circumstances

Introduction

THE LITURGY OF PASTORAL CARE[1]

The word *liturgy* literally means "work," the work of the people of God to be doers of the Word of God. Liturgy, describing the format of worship, highlights both *God's doing* our salvation and *our doing* a response such as caring for suffering people "in the name of the Father and of the Son and of the Holy Spirit."[2] God is always a doer. As Father he brings us life; as Son he gives his own life for us; as Holy Spirit he daily sustains us in the faith. Because God is a doer, he invites us to be doers also, remembering that "our help is in the name of the Lord."[3]

Pastors and those who assist in spiritual care come in peace to suffering people with the message, "The Lord be with you,"[4] and it is said of their visit when they have gone, "This is the Word of the Lord."[5] Pastors and other spiritual caregivers confess the faith, bringing to suffering a holy perspective in words sufferers can hear. Their message is one of hope as they invite those they visit to "lift up your hearts."[6] The reality of every spiritual visit is that two or more are "gathered in the name and the remembrance of Jesus," and they ask Jesus "to forgive, renew, and strengthen us with your Word and Spirit."[7] Some pastoral visits will be a sharing of the body/bread and blood/wine of our Lord so that discouraged people will be able to say, "Oh, give thanks to the Lord, for he is good."[8] And such visits leave sufferers with God's holy mark on their lives: "The Lord bless you and keep you; the Lord make his face shine upon you and be gracious to you... The Lord lift up his countenance on you and give you peace."[9] Such is the liturgy (the work) and the practicality of pastoral care.

Receiving and Doing Pastoral Care

Doing pastoral care toward others begins with having it done to us. But, just as there are people who have never been told by a parent that they are loved, so there are pastors who have never received personal nurturing from another pastor. A pastor of their own childhood may have been cold and aloof, relying solely on the authority of his office to conduct ministry rather than on the love of Christ, which alone ultimately heals wounded souls. Apprenticeship in pastoral care started at the cross when Jesus said to his mother and disciple, "Woman, behold your son," and to the disciple, "Behold, your mother."[10] There Jesus set in motion the generations of pastoral care to follow. God nurtures his people through his people.

I remember one such experience from the early days of my pastoral ministry. I had endured the usual wave of disillusionment that overwhelms every new pastor in discovering that not every parishioner is the incarnation of God's ideal. My expectation of the church as a loving family of faith dissolved quickly. In a God-directed but admittedly rash moment, I decided to leave parish ministry in favor of hospital chaplaincy. As excited and eager as I was to do hospital ministry, I still carried with me the residual pain and grief of the experience of the parish. In the first weeks as a chaplain, in fellowship with a few other chaplains, I experienced the presence, caring, and perspective of God's healing. It happened one day as my grief poured out in front of these chaplains. Their willingness to be with me, the genuineness of their caring, and the holy perspective they brought enabled me to forgive and be forgiven, giving me new life. I learned again through suffering that "all things work together for good to those who love God." With much soul-searching and a deepening of healing I was eventually able to provide the same presence, caring, and perspective for others that God had brought to me. As I had been cared for, God had prepared me to care for others.

PRESENCE, CARING, AND PERSPECTIVE

I use the words "presence," "caring," and "perspective" to describe the aim of pastoral care of sick and suffering people. Each of these words describes an aspect of pastoral care that God works in us. Again, it begins with the cross. As Paul says, "I have been crucified with Christ and I no longer live, but Christ lives in me. The life I live in the body, I live by faith in the Son of God, who loved me and gave himself for me" (Gal. 2:20–21 NIV). We care pastorally for others because Christ, the Good Shepherd of the sheep, cares pastorally for us.

The model of pastoral care I propose is evident in the names by which God reveals himself to us. We come to know how God cared before Jesus was born, for the prophet announced and the angel assured Mary that God's Son was "Emmanuel," which means "God with us."[11] This name announces God's *presence* as the first action of nurturing. God is with us in our suffering! We no longer need to fear being forsaken in suffering. Likewise, the naming of Jesus as "Savior"[12] announces God's action of *caring* "for us ... and for our salvation"[13] on the cross. And the name by which he is ultimately known, "Lord,"[14] assures us that even now he governs all things in holy *perspective* and provides us with the "eyes of faith" to see him at work in our suffering.

God's Nurturing Presence

God's *presence* means God's availability. Many sick and dying people do not feel God is available to them. Either because they have drifted from God and now feel guilty or because they have never known God to be close to them, some feel the vacuous distance all the more in times of illness. Not to be sure of the grace of God toward us at such a time is to be left with a sense of rejection by God. However, God does not leave himself without witness in our suffering; he sends pastors and other caregivers in his name to be his presence to us.

A woman in an Intensive Care Unit called me over to her bedside as I made rounds and said, "Chaplain, we've never met, and I was too weak to speak to you until now, but I want you to know how much seeing you walk by each day gave me comfort in knowing God was with me here in the hospital." She reminded me of the woman who thought, "If I only touch his [Jesus'] garment, I shall be made well."[15] The acknowledged presence of God's people is the acknowledged presence of God.

Pastoral care is the affirmation of God's presence. In the pastor's care of sick and suffering people the greatest presence is the Lord's Supper, where Christ is present in a way that happens nowhere else. In Holy Communion God builds the bridge between heaven and earth so that no separation can exist between physical and spiritual need. In bread and wine, the body and blood of Jesus Christ are present to heal the deeper sickness of the soul, ultimately transforming earthly bodies into eternal ones.

I often wear a clerical collar in the hospital as a sign of God's presence. Christian laity who wear crosses on the lapel or around their neck and who care for the suffering also bear this witness. For some, however, the sight of a pastor in clerical collar or of a Christian wearing a cross may bring forward negative associations. Perhaps they experienced neglect or abuse from a pastor or other Christians. For them the clerical collar or the cross then becomes a barrier. But even this negative association presents pastors with the opportunity to offer nurturing at the foot of the cross, from one wearing the signs of God's presence. God's presence is made known through his people.

God's Caring

"God doesn't care about me; he has forgotten me!" These words are not uncommon from people with chronic or long-term illness. When I ask them whether their nurse or their doctor has been good to them, I am met with an assurance that they have been, while with equal intensity they attest that God has not. Sometimes this intensity is anger toward God that needs to be encouraged to come out, but sometimes the acclaimed absence of God's caring is due to a spiritual ignorance of how God makes himself known. I have said of the care a patient has received from a nurse or doctor, "That's God caring for you. How else would you know whether God cares for you except through people?" I continue, "In fact, that is what God's coming to us in Jesus on the cross is all about; to care for us and our salvation." I am not suggesting that a pastor "preach" rather than listen when he meets with doubt or anger in his parishioners, but he must lead them to see with eyes of faith where God is at work at that moment.

Holy Perspective

Holy perspective is the interpretation of God's presence in the midst of suffering, discovered by pastor and sufferer together when they ask, "Where is God in all of this?" I once visited an elderly hospitalized man by the name of Clarence, whose wife was a cancer patient in our hospital. Clarence had collapsed from exhaustion while visiting her and had to be hospitalized himself. A crusty, tough-minded, retired railroad man, Clarence spoke coarsely of his frustration with his wife's terminal cancer. At one point in his outpouring of complaint I asked, "Where do you see God in all of this?" It always amazes me that people have an answer for this question. Sometimes they say simply, "I don't see God at all in any of this." Whatever answer it generates, the question is as good a starting place as any because it clears the air and allows further exploration together of a holy perspective. But in this case, Clarence knew where he saw God. Holding his fingers two inches apart and in front of my face, he almost shouted, "God is about that big and shrinking all the time." He shared that God had been present in his wife's faithfulness and love for him in spite of his own heavy drinking and carousing in earlier years. However, now as she laying dying, it seemed God was shrinking away from him. In this and subsequent visits Clarence came to know God in other ways, not the least of which was a chaplain's presence and caring for him. I remember saying to him, "I am here as a sign that God is still with you, no matter what may come." He accepted that with "Thank you; I need to hear that."

Holy perspective is not an interpretation by the pastor that tells the sufferer what his suffering means. Rather, the pastor helps the sufferer to verbalize the meaning of his suffering so that together they can find ultimate meaning at the foot of the cross. Helping people discover the presence and caring of God in the midst of their suffering is one of the greatest challenges of pastoral care. Whereas most people look for God in signs of healing for which they have hoped or prayed, few will look on their own for God in suffering.

Refusal to see God in suffering is not a matter of ignorance only but also of resistance. Acknowledging God in the midst of suffering also reduces us to feelings of helplessness and the realization of the loss of control, thus making us dependent on God. Reluctance to be dependent is at the heart of our fear and rebellion against God. Only with the eyes of faith can we see God present in Jesus' suffering on the cross so that resistance is broken down, not by argument or condemnation but by the long-suffering patience and love of God.

It may be difficult to appreciate the impact of a pastor's *presence* in God's name. It may be a little easier to see a pastor's *caring* for others as God's caring. But the pastoral holy *perspective* a pastor brings to the sufferer's situation is the Word of God clearly articulated for the sufferer. Here the sufferer discovers the meaning of his suffering in Christ. Sometimes the impact of a pastor is limited to a quiet presence in God's name. At other times it will include both "presence" and "caring" in Christ's name. But ultimately, pastoral care seeks to help people experience all three together: the presence, the caring, and the holy perspective of God.

An Example
of God's Presence, Caring, and Holy Perspective

Bill had undergone a radical neck dissection to remove a malignant tumor behind his jaw. Few surgeries seem to me to be more uncomfortable and disfiguring than this. I had met Bill shortly before surgery and had assured him of my availability during his hospitalization. A few days after his surgery I was paged while eating lunch and asked to come quickly to Bill's room. When I arrived, I was told that Bill had begun hemorrhaging and, because the cancer was so widespread, the surgeon had chosen not to take Bill back into surgery to stop the bleeding. Bill was bleeding to death in his room, and I was asked to comfort him as he lay dying.

Entering the room, my first sight was of a blood-drenched bed surrounded by nurses packing towels at Bill's neck and chest to absorb the blood that streamed from his ruptured artery. Fully alert, Bill's eyes were filled with terror. He reached out for my hand. I extended mine and was immediately pulled down by him onto the bed amid the blood and debris. Bill's hand held mine so tightly that I soon lost feeling in it. I said little except to attempt to bring the holy perspective: "The Lord is with you, Bill." He seemed to relax a little. (About an hour later, through loss of blood, Bill's bleeding began to slow down and he was taken into surgery after all. Bill survived, to be readmitted to the hospital ten months later, when he died while watching TV a few minutes after he and I had visited.)

Bill had gained a holy perspective on his suffering during that first terror-filled experience. Later he said that he truly had come to know God's presence and caring in the midst of his anguish. My presence and caring were God's presence and caring to him, and he seemed to turn from grasping at life to clinging to the Lord through me. Like the woman following surgery for a brain tumor whose holy perspective enabled her to say "God has been so good to me," Bill too was able to affirm the theology of the cross that God indeed was to be found in the midst of suffering.

FIVE SKILLS OF PASTORAL CARE[16]

Helping people discover the presence, caring, and holy perspective of God in their suffering is an art that begins with the development of pastoral skills. Five skills of pastoral care need to be mastered in order to practice pastoral care well. The first is the skill of nurturing intimacy; second, the skill of encouraging complaint rightly; third, the skill of helping the patient tell a story that includes God; fourth, the skill of sharing suffering appropriately; and finally, the skill of giving comfort from the Gospel.

The Skill of Nurturing Intimacy

To nurture intimacy is to develop a relationship where love is successfully expressed and received, that is, shared. The pastor's love for people reflects God's love for people. Because the latter half of the 20th century unfortunately has given us the understanding of love as an emotion or feeling rather than a calculated commitment to others, it is important for the pastor to model love's intimacy, not as a sensual experience but as a commitment to the life of a suffering parishioner. The commitment to care teaches that God too cares.

The skill of nurturing intimacy is learned through a basic willingness to feel helpless and vulnerable with the parishioner and by refusing to offer simplistic answers, preachy sermons, or distancing maneuvers intended to keep away the pain we are invited to share with the sufferer. This willingness to feel helpless and vulnerable is not the same as feeling inept or unskilled in pastoral care. Helplessness and vulnerability are what a family experiences when, at the bedside of the dying, they realize the inevitable and stop trying to "do" something to maintain control of the situation or of themselves. In such moments the only thing to do is to shed tears and not abandon the dying one. Pastors too at that time may shed holy tears as a sign of God's grief over the wages of sin that leads us all to death's door. At a death it is the pain of the cross that is felt. In time, as the grief passes, it will be the joy of the resurrection that is felt.

This willingness to be and to feel helpless and vulnerable does not come easily and will cost the pastor something emotionally. He will walk away from a visit with the suffering parishioner, and he will feel grief and all its components: anger, sadness, loss, and frustration. Whenever I have come from the bedside following the death of a patient with whom I have shared helplessness and vulnerability, I am drained; yet I cannot help but think it reflects Jesus' exhaustion during his passion. Giving of oneself to others is exhausting, even if there is also renewal in the daily resurrections of remembering who and whose we are and why we do what we do as pastors.

The Skill of Encouraging Complaint

The skill of encouraging complaint consists in eventually directing the patient's legitimate or illegitimate complaint away from illness, treatment, doctors, or anything else to focus on the helplessness and loss of control behind the complaint, so that it can be brought to God. The temptation many sympathetic pastors succumb to when suffering people complain is either to join in, adding their own litany of similar experiences, or else to defend the one being attacked, be that the doctor, nurse, or hospital. It needs to be said that the sufferer may have an entirely legitimate reason to criticize the doctor, the hospital, or the system of health care; but the pastor's task at this point is not to act either as patient advocate or defender of the persecuted. Instead, encourage the complaint so that it can be redirected to God. A well-meaning pastor warned an angry mother not to blame God for her son's illnesses, but the astute woman responded, "Whom else can I go to with my complaint if not to God?" Such a complaint is not the whining type that required God to justify himself but rather the terrified complaint of a woman whose only son was dying. The pastor's task is to help the parishioner take his complaints to the throne of heaven so that like Job in pouring out the pain, he might find peace.

The Skill of Helping to Tell a Story

Worn down by sickness, the suffering parishioner may at times conclude that life is chaotic and random, having no coherent meaning to it. The danger exists that, believing life to be meaningless, the parishioner will miss seeing God's part in all that has been happening and be unable to tell a personal story of his experience that includes God. The purpose of the parishioner's putting together such a story (with the pastor's help) is to answer the question, "Where is God in all of this?" Although life may seem random, the prolog of our personal story begins with God creating us, and the epilog concludes with God's promise of eternal life. The task of the sufferer is to put together the pieces of his life in such a way that it satisfies him as he tells a coherent story of his suffering.

My father took 80 years to put his story together. When he was five years old in New York City at the turn of the 20th century, he and his family had planned to attend a Sunday school picnic on the paddleboat *Slocum*. When that day came, my father was sick and unable to go, so he and his parents stayed home while hundreds of others, including nearly all his relatives, boarded the *Slocum* to travel up the Hudson River to Bear Mountain. History records that the *Slocum* caught fire and sank, killing over 300 people, including most of my father's relatives. The question "Why was I spared" haunted my father. Finally, in his 80s, Dad said to me one

Sunday after church, "You know, I think the reason I was spared was so that I could have you and you could be a pastor." For the first time, Dad saw God's hand in his personal story of tragedy, and he concluded, "All things work together for good to those that love God." It is this "all things working for good" at the hands of God that every sufferer must identify in order to tell a story that will sustain him. The skill of helping the sufferer tell a story of suffering that includes God comes through patient listening and gently raising the question, "Where do you see the hand of God in all of this?"

The Skill of Sharing Suffering

Sometimes the task of the pastor is not to relieve or take away suffering but to share it. This is not a contradiction to the church's history of creating hospitals and institutions of mercy that relieve pain and suffering but another aspect of pastoral care. Here pastoral care follows the ministry of Jesus, who "has borne our grief and carried our sorrows." The goal of this sharing of suffering is to enable the sufferer to see God through the pastor's bearing of grief and carrying of sorrow. A thin line exists between the pastoral skill of nurturing intimacy (of which we spoke earlier) and this sharing of suffering. Nurturing intimacy encourages the sufferer to love and trust God. Sharing suffering helps the sufferer to interpret his relationship to God, recognizing that God is for him and not against him.

When the pastor allows himself to suffer with the sufferer, he preaches the theology of the cross most boldly. The pastor says in effect, "God comes to us in weakness and in suffering. Let us watch for him." It took six months of sitting at the bedside of Elizabeth, an arrogant, successful, yet cancer-ridden attorney, before we discovered God's presence in her suffering. As I visited Elizabeth nearly every day during her stay in the hospital, I frequently felt helpless, useless, and unwanted. Somehow, though, it seemed important to bear with the callous, hostile facade of this dying lady. It was at the end of her life, after she had been discharged briefly from and finally readmitted to the hospital, that we together discovered God's presence. Humbled by God through her illness, Elizabeth confessed, "You know, I hated to see you come each day. Just seeing you reminded me I was going to die, and I didn't want to face that. But I know you meant well and you cared, and I want to thank you." She then related how she had come to faith in the interim between hospitalizations. We prayed together, she and I, one in Christ.

The goal of sharing suffering is to help the sufferer learn to see God.

The Skill of Comforting

Comforting is not simply a matter of making a suffering person feel better. Often pastoral comfort is preceded by discomfort for the sufferer as she struggles to come to terms with her illness. Patients who begin to pour out resentment or sorrow feel uncomfortable because it hurts. Pastors who rush in to relieve that pain, either out of motives of compassion or righteous indignation, may close a wound that still needs to be drained. Likewise, sufferers who struggle against illness or even against God need to be permitted the discomfort of their anger and denial before they can honestly face illness, death, or God. Elizabeth's admission of her "hating to see me each time I came in" needed to come out, even if it was hard for her to say and hard for me to hear, for she needed to confess her sins. We diminish the integrity of the person's confession and discomfort when we say, "No problem; forget it." What the sufferer needs to hear is not our waving away her discomfort but our voicing acceptance and forgiveness in Christ.

The pastor's temporary silence at hearing discomforting things does not necessarily mean he condones their complaint or distorted perspective. A postponed response to his impulse to set things straight for the sake of comforting the sufferer allows the pastor to listen carefully for more of the problem behind the discomfort. Surely every pastor has discovered a parishioner who needs his discomfort until he has arrived at an appropriate solution of his own making.

The goal of pastoral care is not necessarily to remove a person's discomfort, but to help the sufferer use the discomfort for growth in faith and love of God. Elizabeth's discomfort at my daily presence in her life was a reminder of the need to pay attention to God in the midst of her suffering, something she was trying hard not to do. Ultimately, her discomfort contributed to her final comfort in Christ. God comes not just in our comfort but in our discomfort as well.

THE STRUCTURE OF A VISIT

Much of the success of pastoral care depends on the structure of the visit and the timing of our words. What may be appropriate to say or do in the abstract may not fit an actual situation. It may be helpful to think of the pastoral visit in four segments: (1) an introduction to set the tone of the visit; (2) clarification of the purpose of the visit, which then develops into (3) the content of the visit; and, (4) a skilled termination of the visit. Also, a pastoral visit usually begins superficially, then deepens, and then becomes superficial again. Initially, the patient may be caught off guard by a pastoral caregiver's visit, perhaps wondering, "Why is he here?"

The introduction to a visit ought to include not only the visitor's name (some parishioners who have been delinquent do not remember how to pronounce the new pastor's name), but also with a proposal for some common ground on which to begin the visit. Often this proposal consists in discussion of the weather, a baseball game, or something else they have in common. This proposal for a superficial start allows each to feel at ease with the visit and eases the threat/comfort dichotomy which God's presence always produces.

The problem is that this introduction segment often never progresses to the next segment, and pastors come away feeling that nothing happened in the visit. Some pastors resort to having a Bible reading or prayer at this point for lack of something happening in the visit. Although a shared devotion is almost always appropriate, the pastor needs to learn how to move the visit from a superficial to a deepened level of discussion. This happens in the pastor's clarification of the purpose of his visit (as generic as that purpose may be), as in, "I was concerned about you and wanted to see how you are doing." This genuine invitation to tell the pastor how things are going gives opportunity for the sufferer to share his/her life with the pastor at a deeper level.

The content of the visit, the third segment, consists in expression of feelings and thoughts. When a sufferer pours out feelings in the form of tears, anger, or other emotion, the pastor would do well not to interrupt. Interrupting strong emotions will almost always block the parishioner's further openness at that moment. The message conveyed by the pastor in his interruption is, "The pastor wants me to stop this emotional outpouring, so I had better not say more."

When the flow of emotion is completed, the patient may, with the pastor's help, move from the intensity of feelings to reflective thought. Sufferers need to move from feelings to thought in order to deepen their understanding of life with God. Learning as well as catharsis needs to take place, and teaching is always a part of pastoral care of the sick.

The fourth and final segment of a pastoral visit, the conclusion, is most critical in pastoral care. The termination of the visit must help the sufferer tie up loose ends, if only by handing everything over to God until future resolution of problems can be attained.

In concluding the visit, review what the visit has been about, thus giving affirmation to the patient who may have second thoughts about what they told the pastor. I have had patients actually ask me, "Is it okay that I told you these things?" They are asking if they used the visit appropriately. "Was it okay that I cried or that I said things that betray my fears or desires?" Assure them that this is acceptable, that taking you into their confidence is appropriate.

One of the elements of terminating the visit might be prayer, in which the pastor pulls together the loose ends of the visit (but not introducing things you did not talk about), both as a summary and as a way to commend all things to God. I like to think of a prayer at the close of a visit as a way of handing the person over to God as I leave. Only under extreme circumstances does a pastor want to leave the patient feeling at loose ends. The pastor will want to help the patient resume his day with the added renewal of their visit and the blessing, "Go in peace; serve the Lord."

5

Crossing the Years:
The Elderly

What does it mean to be old? Although it may be difficult for us to identify a time when it begins, there are days as adults when we realize we are aging. As a 79-year-old friend complains that she is becoming forgetful, I admit that already at age 55 I cannot remember things as well as I did in my 20s. She refuses to hear this, protesting, "You're too young to forget!" Nevertheless, by the time we reach the age of 40 we have all been made aware that waning vitality is calling us toward a mellower pace (which feels more comfortable to us every passing day). But, as my father used to say, even in his 90s after a full evening of dancing with mother in her 80s, "You're only as young as you feel." I suspect that for some, even when a person is no longer physically able to dance, there is still a child inside that feels young on at least some days.

For our purposes, although barely a conclusion to the middle years, age 65 will be the benchmark of what we identify as the beginning of being "older," since at this age retirement has begun—a new phase of life that will be increasingly characterized by the problems of aging. Age 65 and older is recognized by hospital administrators as the age of the largest group of patients. In parish planning meetings, pastors speak of parishioners this age as retirees, and it is recognized that in a few more years visiting these will be a major part of the pastor's ministry. Although advances in medicine offer life to many who would have died much earlier, the fact is that most will die even older, but with the same diseases that have been delayed thus far: cancer and heart disease.

Ministry to the chronically-ill elderly requires an appreciation for the theology of the cross, for it is here we see God's strength made perfect in weakness. Recognizing his own mortality, C. S. Lewis put it well in writing to an old friend: "Yes, autumn is really the best of the seasons; and I'm not sure that old age isn't the best part of life. But, of course, like autumn, it doesn't last."[1] Being elderly is the usual preliminary for dying.

Some years before the advent of minimally-invasive surgery, a 100-year-old woman in critical need of a surgeon's attention to her gall bladder lay in our Intensive Care Unit. The surgeon, reluctant to do surgery because of her age, tried to convince the patient to consider, instead, analgesics and a comfortable surrender of her life to this illness. But looking into the eyes of what must have seemed to her a boy by comparison, the old woman said, "Young man, in three months I will be 101 years old. I want to live to see that birthday." She was operated on, recovered, and lived to see that birthday—and more.

Is there a point when we as a society should stop offering the elderly medical care and life? Some societies today have done so, and we shall speak more of this in a later chapter on medical ethics. For now the question is, "Is pastoral care of the elderly-sick only a matter of comfort, or are there deeper pastoral challenges to meet even for this group of patients?"

THE ELDERLY TODAY

Who are these elderly today who increasingly make up a larger and larger share of our population and how can we continue to care for their spiritual growth in sickness and in health?

We are told by demographics experts, the elderly make up an increasingly larger portion of the population than any other age group. Yet, because the elderly are out of the mainstream of the business world, we seldom consider them movers and shakers of our world. Business may see them as a market for making money, but business seldom seeks the wisdom, experience, or perspective · of the elderly. In fact, the elderly are perceived as the source of a problem for themselves and for others who fear these will exhaust the Social Security system and burden the remaining few with enormous health care costs. Others fear the elderly will become a personal burden of time and attention because they require the care of loved ones.

Sadly, we live in a culture that increasingly sees the elderly as a burden rather than an asset. Therefore, it is important for the church to challenge our culture to protect the elderly, to both enhance self-worth, and to call the rest of us to a willingness to bear the burden of caring for the elderly. In a culture that measures self-worth by what we produce, the church offers a counter message that human worth has more to do with what God has done for us on the cross and in our Baptism than with what we manage to achieve or produce in life. The elderly remind us all that we live by grace and not by human merit. In short, the elderly are a reminder of the theology of the cross, which alone gives fulfillment to our lives.

The Elderly as Servants of Christ

Unfortunately, many of the elderly in our churches today are more content to make trips to Las Vegas, play bingo, or attend social events sponsored by the congregation than they are to participate in the vital life of the church. Perhaps because they see themselves as deserving freedom from responsibilities and obligations and are drawn to the love of leisure, they excuse themselves from serious consideration in important planning and participation in parish life. And if they become ill or leave to spend the winter in Florida, they may think twice about serious involvement in the church.

The elderly, however, even with their times of incapacity or travel, are a treasure for the church. They have a unique perspective to offer others on the significance of spiritual life, for they have begun to formulate for themselves how years of grace are fulfilling God's plan for them.

In the challenges presented to pastoral care there is opportunity to help the elderly pull together many loose threads of their lives so that what emerges is a witness to and resource for others who need a wiser person with a larger perspective on life in times of trouble and hardship. In short, pastoral care not only aims to comfort the elderly but challenges them to see themselves as resources of wisdom and faith. Pastoral care calls the elderly to give the rest of us a perspective that only they have, they who have come full circle from birth to heaven's door.

DEVELOPMENTAL ASPECTS OF THE ELDERLY[2]

If the elderly are to be a source of wisdom and people to whom we turn, something must happen along life's way before they are old to make them such. Wisdom and holy perspective do not begin spontaneously at old age; these virtues begin with the holy perspective that God gives along the whole path of life. It is essential that we continually grow spiritually from youth through old age, learning to understand ourselves and others in relation to God. We must learn to love God and other people, and finally to love God more than any other person.

Personal development begins with what we receive from our parents, but along the way depends more and more on the choices we make, using what our families have given us for better or for worse. In infancy, we are faced with learning the balance between trust and mistrust, knowing when to trust completely and when to question. In our life with God this forms a balance between trusting God absolutely and bringing to God in all honesty the doubts we have about his trustworthiness. Where else can we go when we doubt another's love except to the one whose love we need the most?

Our next developmental task is to learn the balance between being an individual and having a healthy doubt about our self-sufficiency. We are more than an extension of our parent's lives; God has made us individuals, responsible ultimately to him alone. At the same time, a healthy sense of doubt about our own omnipotence helps us recognize our need for others and ultimately for God.

A third developmental task of early life involves learning to take initiative while maintaining a healthy sense of limits—even experiencing guilt when we have gone or are tempted to go too far. This developmental task ensures that we will be able to take reasonable risks in life and also to know when to pull back in repentance when those risks involve us in dangerous, sinful behavior.

In the early years of our growing up, we need to develop confidence in our competency to perform basic tasks of daily living such as learning skills or being able to communicate well. At the same time we must learn the limits of our particular skills and accept them contentedly. If we hold an exaggerated sense of our own capabilities, we may find it hard to imagine grace at work in our lives. A knowledge of our limits enhances the awareness of grace and eventually moves us from satisfaction centered on achievements to enjoyment of relationships. This is one of the chief characteristics of growing older, namely, that we move from "things" to people. It is here that wisdom is shared with young people and friendship with friends.

In adolescence we spend much of our time trying to find out who we are. The goal is to identify, apart from parents and the world we have known, who we are for ourselves, yet in relationship to God. Although young people need to separate identity from parents, they sometimes break the relationship completely and, in doing so, also break the relationship with God. But there is reconciliation to be had with both—and this too is part of growing up in Christ. In order to grow wise as we grow older, we must come to see our identity as a child of God and recognize ourselves as creatures under God as Creator.

Further development precipitating the onset of a good old age is the development of the capacity for a paradox of intimacy and solitude. On the one hand, we must learn to enjoy the closeness of people we can talk with and listen to; and on the other, we need to develop a peacefulness in times of solitude.

This puts us in a good position to share our wisdom as a gift to others. Even in my 50s I occasionally long for a talk with some older soldier of the cross who will help me think through my own life in a way that brings me again and again to the foot of the cross and to the peace found there. The need for mentors continues throughout life, pointing us to God as the only one who finally meets our needs.

Assuming dementia or other cognitive problems do not interfere with development in old age, the arrival at peaceful resolution to our lives and contentedness is the desired goal of life. Pastoral care along the way and into old age can help a person arrive there. If this does not occur, there will likely be some degree of despair. At this point, there is little left to do but to assure the elderly of God's redeeming grace and to comfort them with God's presence, caring, and the perspective that life hereafter will be better. Elderly people who have not developed trust, autonomy, industriousness, identity, capacity for intimacy, or who have not

82

served others will find it virtually impossible to experience a contented ending to their lives. Nevertheless, "with God all things are possible." Grace extends to the end. God never gives up on us, and we dare not abandon one another; for God so loved the world that he sent his Son to redeem it.

Pastoral Care of the Storyteller Elderly

Pastors and other spiritual caregivers need to understand themselves as growing older in order to understand the needs of the elderly. As we have suggested earlier, all of us need to make as much sense of our lives as we possibly can, and we need to verbalize our understanding in a story that includes both God and those experiences of suffering that can make or break us. (Even by itself, aging can be an experience of suffering, since it demands much in the way of accepting the limits of our bodies and minds.)

How can we help the elderly tell their story? Begin by developing patience to listen long. Pastors sometimes grow weary of elderly people who tell of past events in great repetitive detail at each visit; but it takes months—even years—to get the story right, and it is not as though nothing is happening during listening. To be sure, there are exceptions to the rule in listening long, such as when the elderly simply speak because they are lonely and don't want you to leave, or, they have lost all memory of what was said before. As the pastor makes a judgement call whether or not to listen, he must realize that talking about one's life is critical for the elderly. The pastor's part is to continue asking, "Where do you see God in all of that?" This question helps the elderly tell the whole story instead of dwelling on their suffering. In his letter to the believers in Rome, St. Paul tells his own story and reminds us, "We rejoice in our sufferings, knowing that suffering produces endurance, and endurance produces character, and character produces hope, and hope does not disappoint us, because God's love has been poured into our hearts through the Holy Spirit which has been given to us."[3]

Pastoral Care of the Grieving Elderly

Aging is a process in which the elderly grieve the losses that occur every day. Not only do they lose spouse, family, and friends in death, but they also lose abilities and physical strength. Movement, safety, habits, memory—those things young people take for granted—begin to elude elderly people. As they grieve these losses, older people may despair, especially if they have no story that makes sense of their losses. For the Christian, even losses point to something more hopeful. At the core of our loss is the reminder from St. Paul: "While we were yet helpless, at the right time Christ died for the ungodly."[4]

The theology of the cross becomes more comforting when we accept our weakness as the opportunity for God's strength in us. If the ultimate loss in life is death, then for the Christian it is gain, since it relieves us of weakness and puts on us a glorious strength that only God can give. All other losses in aging are reminders of this, and instead of despair there is a growing hope that things will be better in the Lord's "right time." Pastors can be helpful to the elderly by acknowledging complaints of personal loss and not trying to comfort them by talking them out of their grieving but walking with them through it. The difficulty is that pastors sometimes are so busy with mundane tasks that they think time spent with the elderly is an interruption; and yet this is the kind of task to which we are called. Pastors are the hand of God that touches the elderly gently in their grief and, from the foot of the cross, beckons them to look up to Christ, where loss becomes victory. In helping the elderly to grieve the death of a spouse or adult child, the pastor gently and patiently challenges them to learn to love God more than those they have lost, so that hope for eternity is focused on God first and loved ones second.

Pastoral Care of the Elderly Dependent

In our culture, dependency is thought to be an evil to be avoided at all costs. We may wrestle with the fine distinctions between dependency, interdependency, and codependency, but the bottom line is that we fear and try to avoid being dependent on anyone. This fear is behind some of the hostility toward doctors and the medical establishment, since medicine reminds us that sickness and dying make us dependent. Ultimately such dependency on people also reminds us of our dependency on God. For the elderly man who has been a self-made and self-reliant person all his life, bowing the knee before God can be more than a problem of arthritis. For the elderly woman who has taken care of others all her life, giving up control and allowing others to care for her can be more than a fear of bed rest.

Pastors can help the elderly learn to see dependency as something they have lived with all their lives and didn't know it. The elderly dependent need to see life from the holy perspective that what they thought was their independence throughout life was really grace extended generously. We all resist dependency on God; it is part of the sinfulness of human nature. But pastors can help the elderly detach enough from self and the culture in order to teach younger generations by example how to graciously depend on others. Dependency at the foot of the cross is a relief and a joy, for in weakness we find strength. In that strength we have overcome the human fear of dependency. As the elderly come to this wisdom, they have much to teach those who care for them, for God says, "My [strength] is made perfect in weakness."[5]

Pastoral Care of the Vulnerable Elderly

While my parents were retired on the east coast of Florida, I used to say (in my cynical moments) that two kinds of people lived there: those elderly who have enough money to do so and those younger who are trying to get that money away from the elderly.

The elderly are a constant prey to others who take advantage of them, and it is understandable that paranoia can be characteristic of the elderly at times. For example, the adult children of a prosperous, elderly woman who was a patient in our hospital came to our ethics committee with a bold request: "We'd like you to help us end the life of our mother." Later we learned that they had attempted the same with their father. The elderly are vulnerable— and at times need protection even from those responsible for caring for them. Increasingly, the suggestion is heard that one way to cut health care costs is to cut short the lives of the elderly. Pastors may have to play a prophetic as well as a pastoral role in intervening for their elderly parishioners.

Because the elderly are vulnerable due to slowness or due to loss of judgement because of memory impairment, pastors need to help them accept help and draw others in as younger friends who can assist them. My wife and I, for example, cared for our children's piano teacher into her 90s. Appreciative, she would often ask my wife, "Why do you do this?" It was then that my wife had opportunity to say, "Because God loves you and I love you."

Pastoral Care of the Self-Centered Elderly

In old age, life seems to shrink back into the self as we are left alone after friends and family die and solitude becomes more and more acceptable. Because tasks such as cooking, eating, bathing, and other basic activities demand so much time and energy, little is left for interaction with others outside the home. Even in nursing homes, residents sometimes seldom leave their rooms except to eat and to comply with planned activities. As a result, the elderly may seem preoccupied with themselves and can appear demanding as they are unaware of the demands of time on others. For this reason the pastoral visit becomes a focal point of life for many.

I recall visiting an elderly woman in my first parish who seemed to live for my visits each week. I would usually find her sitting on her bed in the nursing home wearing her best dress, hair combed, eager eyes fixed on the door, awaiting my entrance. The nurses told me it was clearly the highlight of her week and the reason she kept going.

With forced attention on the self due to the amount of energy demanded to tend life's basic tasks, the elderly can lose perspective and become extreme in some aspect of their personality. Formerly generous people can become demanding. Cheerful people can become angry over trivial things. Like young children, they expect the world to revolve around them and complain that they get no attention from their children (even when the children call daily or visit several times a week).

It is helpful to the elderly who demand more than is appropriate to set limits for them and for those who care for them. The pastor who sets a regular day to visit and keeps that appointment provides a bright light in the older person's life. By directing their hopes more and more away from preoccupation with trivial concerns of self-care, the pastor moves attention to God's care of them in their frustration and helplessness. The aspects of presence and caring in God's name as well as supporting the holy perspective they struggle to maintain is all part of the care of the elderly.

A HOLY PERSPECTIVE ON THE SEASONS OF LIFE FOR THE ELDERLY

The seasons of the year, especially in a northern climate, help to view life and especially old age from God's perspective, a holy perspective. Winter, spring, summer, and fall bear their own reminders of life's journey and of God's grace in Christ. In winter's bleakness, when everything seems to die, God gives life. A Child is born! This is the theology of the crèche and cross: in sickness and loss we experience the presence, caring, and perspective of God. In spring, when life springs from the earth, God gives us Good Friday and his Son's death on the cross. Life springs from death. So also, the elderly can say with Paul, "For to me ... to die is gain." In summer when instead of recreation and vacations the elderly may be dealing with chronic illness and growing weakness, God's love in Christ still radiates from the cross. And in autumn, when the world anticipates fading greenery and winter's death, God points our eyes beyond death to eternal life. Things are not as they seem when viewed with physical eyes alone. The death and resurrection of Jesus Christ has turned all things upside down; a new creation has begun also for the elderly.

With the Aid of the Cross: AIDS[1]

If aging is not a disease yet eventually brings us to death's door, AIDS represents the darker side of our fallen nature, the side that both brings us face to face with death and is associated with behavior for which Christ offers forgiveness and reconciliation. That is, AIDS is predominantly spread by promiscuity, either homosexual or heterosexual, and by illicit drug use. AIDS spreads as the "wages of sin" in a fallen world.

True—it is important to note the personal innocence of infants born with AIDS, wives who are the victims of unfaithful husbands, those who contract AIDS through blood transfusions, and others infected through no fault of their own. Yet AIDS is still spread predominantly by sexual promiscuity and represents the collective sinfulness of a fallen world. We live in a sinful world, but a world to which God calls Christians to minister. We do so in order that those who sit in darkness might see the light, namely Christ's cross and the presence, caring, and perspective it brings to our lives.

There are two possibilities that seem to allow us to avoid the issues that AIDS raises. Either God in his grace will grant a cure for AIDS and we will not have to struggle with the issues, or AIDS will continue and will be viewed as a disease divorced from moral behavior. The latter is already happening. Under pressure from relativistic and pluralistic values, many have suspended judgement and chosen not to look at these issues or the crises of faith that AIDS presents. But AIDS presents a crisis of faith for pastor and patient alike. The pastor is faced with the choice between urging repentance or remaining silent, and the promiscuous AIDS patient is faced with the choice between repenting or rejecting repentance. Those who offer pastoral care are to "love the sinner, but hate the sin." It would be a relief to pastors to not have to deal with AIDS and its moral implications, but it would be a sin to see AIDS as merely a biological process divorced from moral accountability. The opportunity to discover life as God intended it to be lived in wholeness of body and spirit is at stake. Most discussions of AIDS omit this kind of spiritual care. This chapter, therefore, will attempt to help the pastor relate Christ's love as expressed in the theology of the cross to those with AIDS in need of God's presence, caring, and perspective.

AIDS: WITHOUT THE AID OF THE CROSS

The first case of AIDS was reported in this country in 1982. In the ten years following, AIDS led to 150,000 deaths and another 220,000 persons infected with the HIV virus. It is reported that the United States has the highest number of AIDS cases, some 70% of the world's total.[2] Although initially presented as a disease among homosexuals in this country, in Africa AIDS is presented as a heterosexual disease, growing most rapidly in burgeoning urban areas where traditional values break down under social change and where prostitutes become the major transmitter of AIDS.[3]

The human response to AIDS has spanned the spectrum from compassion to neutrality to hostility. In the early years of the AIDS discovery, the nursing department in our hospital instinctively turned to the homosexual community to tell us how to respond.

But it is a false assumption that those who experience something are the experts who know how to deal with it. We were misled when the homosexual community told us that germs, not lifestyle, cause AIDS. Still today, few challenge this moral evasion for fear of being accused of homophobia or sexual bias. We sublimate the intuition which red-flags this erroneous simplistic explanation. As attention turns to "infection control," moral questions are laid aside. AIDS patients are treated the same as patients with other infectious diseases. As a result, the need for reconciliation is ignored, and AIDS patients are not cared for spiritually. Clearly, the issue of moral accountability and the need for reconciliation are passed over. The question "Where is God in all of this" is dismissed as a judgmental attitude in need of cure like the disease itself.

A Word about Homosexuality

Homosexuality has been around since ancient times but has never been acceptable as a Judeo-Christian ethic. Its rejection by Christians is based on an understanding of the distinction made by God between male and female and the corresponding reality of Christ and his church as bride and groom. In Romans 1, St. Paul associates homosexual behavior with the fallenness of the world, a distortion of the faithfulness to which we are called as men and women in Christ.

There is much discussion today about the origins of homosexuality, but there is no clear, objective evidence that finds homosexuality to be something in the genes or, for that matter, anything physically different from heterosexuality. Some hope to find a homosexual chromosome that would allow them to claim homosexuality as acceptable sexual expression. Others fear the discovery of such a chromosome because the discovery will lead, as one homosexual said, to "curing it as if it were a disease." But the issue of origin or physiology of homosexuality is irrelevant for Christians, since our source of moral guidance is the Word of God, not science.

Freud was the first to propose the idea of an orientation called "homosexual." Prior to Freud, homosexual behavior was associated with deviant heterosexual behavior as far back as ancient Greece, where it was encouraged in the military in order to create loyalty between soldiers who would be expected to fight alongside and in defense of their lovers. It may be that Freud created something that doesn't exist except in so far as culture creates it, namely the "homosexual personality." In any case, a so-called homosexual orientation is still a part of the fallenness of this world, and the behavior that acts it out is still a matter of moral choice. The homosexual Christian who chooses celibacy is to be supported and respected. The church needs to say publicly that homosexual behavior is sinful, while pastorally reaching out in love to men and women who need God's grace in Jesus Christ to change their lives.

AIDS and *Hetero*sexuals

Not all AIDS patients are homosexuals. Some are children or spouses or blood recipients with feelings of anger and betrayal. Pastoral care of these does not focus on the need to repent of a lifestyle but on the need to forgive an unfaithful spouse or those in a health care system who may have caused the spread of AIDS. Ultimately, these patients may have to be helped to face their anger at God. Anger seems to be the predominant and understandable response, but it can turn to a bitterness that requires pastoral care.

WHERE IS GOD IN ALL OF THIS?

The question remains for every pastor or spiritual caregiver who understands the good life God intends for us and who desires to provide spiritual care to AIDS patients: "Where is God in all of this?" The Law of God sets limits, showing us our sin and pointing us to God; while the Gospel offers forgiveness and reconciliation in Christ. Both are ingredients of pastoral care, although appropriate timing and sensitivity to people in speaking truth is critical. Moral accountability is part of the message of pastoral care wherever promiscuity, adultery, or homosexual behavior are part of life; but it is the Gospel which gives life. Speaking the truth in love sometimes takes the form of "tough love," which may appear to be rejection but is really outreach to include sinners under God's canopy of grace, the ultimate goal for pastoral care to AIDS patients. But it is extremely delicate and difficult to know how to speak the truth in love to AIDS patients so that it is heard properly and truthfully by them.

Case in Point

I received a request from a newly-diagnosed AIDS patient to visit him at my leisure. This message conveyed no sense of urgency and, indeed, hinted at the patient's ambivalence in asking for a pastor. He explained that he had been watching television and had heard a TV evangelist say that all homosexuals are going to hell. "Is this true?" he asked me with sincere concern.

Speaking the truth in love required a response that assured him of grace while at the same time did not condone his sin. Since it is often helpful to wait with relief even for the penitent lest they bury deeper needs, I asked him, "Tell me, what it is you are worried about with God?" He then expressed self-doubts, revealing guilt about his homosexual lifestyle. I knew from previous experience that agreeing too quickly might be overwhelming, so I encouraged him to go on. He talked, not directly about homosexuality but about promiscuity, and I supported his repentance.

The common ground of our need for forgiveness, whether homosexual or heterosexual, puts us together at the foot of the cross. I have always believed that the more we can draw in common on the need for God's grace, the more we will find it together in Christ. This attitude does not minimize the sinfulness of a homosexual lifestyle, but it prevents us from becoming self-righteous.

It has been my experience in working with AIDS patients that, as homosexuals, these men share certain traits of which pastors should be aware. For example, homosexuals are frequently immature emotionally (often on the level of an early adolescent), preoccupied with sexual identity, rebellious against parents, and rejecting of all authority. They are isolated and alienated from the community, their families, and the church, preferring instead the company of peers.

The entrance of a pastor into the life of a young, hospitalized AIDS patient at the point of life's greatest threat is often overwhelming to the patient. It takes more patience and compassion to reach out in truth and love than with other parishioners. The parish pastor who is asked by parents to visit a homosexual son in the hospital faces a negative association in the son's mind even before the visit begins. The burden of proof lies on us to love them past their apprehension, suspicion, and outright hostility.

Faith before Change

Since the pastoral care of homosexuals with AIDS is a difficult challenge for most pastors, let me share my own journey towards such pastoral care. I have met several young men who, as homosexuals, either have chosen to live a celibate life or have tried to reject their homosexuality altogether and to find support for a new life. I learned, however, that these young men seldom experience love and frequently seek its substitute in sexual encounters in spite of their plans. They most often are alienated from parents and others not homosexual; and even in the liaisons between homosexuals, fickle exchange of partners is frequent. So, I resolved to work at loving these young men, giving them a model of wholesome love apart from sexual associations. I tried to "love" them into the arms of God.

Love, however, needs a name; and it soon became evident that faith in Jesus Christ is the truth that needs to be spoken in love. Without it, love is mistaken for many things, not the least of which is a condoning of the homosexual. It is a mistake for us to expect a homosexual to listen to our belief that homosexuality is part of the fallenness of this world without his first having the faith to comprehend this. Therefore, as with anyone living in rebellion against God, faith must precede any expected change based on an appeal to Christian values. Faith comes before change, since it is the Spirit of God, not human compassion that transforms broken lives. It is always the task of pastoral care first to present the Christian faith rather than merely expect behavioral changes per se. To do otherwise is to become moralistic and judgmental. The Spirit of God is at work in the presence, caring, and perspective that we bring, and the seed of faith is planted when the Word of God is spoken.

PASTORAL CARE OF PARENTS OF AIDS CHILDREN

Parents do not expect children to die before they do. In the case of AIDS and homosexuality, there is most often a period of alienation in which the son is lost to parents for years prior to hospitalization for AIDS, which brings them face to face again. Occasionally, parents are unaware that the son is living a homosexual lifestyle and the double diagnosis of lifestyle and AIDS is devastating.

Parents may react in several ways. Fathers often become angry and find reconciliation difficult. Mothers more likely will be accepting and unconditional in their love. Both parents will often search their hearts and parenting skills and ask, "What did we do that went wrong?" It is at this point that public attitude toward AIDS and acceptance of homosexuality offers them a poor escape route. Parents may choose not to deal with their anger at their son (or with their guilt) and simply accept the disease as any other disease, paying little attention to the wrenching hurt and loss that preceded it for both them and their son.

It is helpful for the pastor to sit down with these parents alone in their homes and encourage them to talk about these things. Lead-ing them to discover forgiveness toward a son is better than talking them into being tolerant. Frequently the alienation between parents and children has a long history, and the pastor's visits might have to continue into the period of grieving following the son's death. It is crucial for the pastor to be close at hand in order to walk with the parents through the crises and the dying. The parents need to find healing in the Word of God and resist joining the ranks of those parents who have nothing to comfort them but tolerance.

SUICIDE AND THE CROSS

The ethic of suicide will be discussed in a later chapter on depression, but for now we look at the pastoral care of those AIDS patients who consider suicide as an answer to their problem. Needless to say, there are others with chronic or terminal illnesses who also take their own lives, but the AIDS patient is especially vulnerable because of the stigma and isolation AIDS creates. It must be said first that any AIDS patient who hints at suicide should be taken seriously, since the homosexual community has romanticized suicide, calling it a "rational" response to the prospect of suffering and death from AIDS. As with all who are suicidal, all threats should be taken seriously. Those who provide pastoral care should also be aware of the possibility of manipulation by threats of self harm. Jesus urges us to be "wise as serpents and innocent as doves," but the practical wisdom of responding to suicidal threats takes precedence. A pastor who attempts to prevent an AIDS patient from committing suicide must not blame himself if the patient succeeds. Those who want to take their own lives will find a way to do so regardless.

Nevertheless, there are some preventive measures that are helpful. Take all threats seriously. Do not minimize threats, but let the patient know you believe he could do such a thing if so desired. Make it clear that you do not want him to do such a thing. In fact, it is sometimes enough to prevent a suicide by asking the person to promise not to harm himself, but promise to meet again. Fourth, if the patient is depressed and seems unable to actively respond to this, try putting him in touch with a psychiatrist who will prescribe antidepressants. Depression, as we shall see in another chapter, is not usually something a person can be "talked out of." Any request on the patient's part for you to keep the threat of suicide a secret should be rejected. Promises of self-harm or harm to others ought not be included in the confidentiality of a visit, and the patient should be told so when secrecy is asked for. Whatever anger the AIDS patient may have for this breaking of confidentiality will hopefully be seen also as concern for the patient's welfare rather than as a betrayal of confidence.

If the AIDS patient has managed to get a doctor to assist in suicide by prescribing a lethal supply of drugs, you can still ask the patient not to do so. Your beneficent authority means a lot. Although you cannot ultimately prevent suicide, your concern, motivated by love, is a powerful and needed corrective to a sense of isolation and abandonment by others. All it sometimes takes to enable a person to live is for one other person to care. If that person is a Christian caregiver who tells of the spiritual consequences of suicide, the patient will have even more reason to think twice. I have frequently been asked by people contemplating suicide whether they will go to hell if they commit suicide; they tell me that the only reason they didn't kill themselves was the fear of damnation. I never give way to false assurances of understanding on God's part that take away inhibitions toward suicide. To do so is easily mistaken for permission. AIDS patients cry out for help, express fear and anger, and feel alone when they threaten suicide. Pastoral care by a loving, sensitive, and firm pastor will offer more than anything else. At the same time the AIDS patient may need to express anger toward God by directing it at the pastor. Such anger needs to be taken as a cry for help and needs to be responded to with pastoral counseling. To whom else can we go when we are angry other than to God? The pastor's response to the suicidal AIDS patient will have to take the form of a commitment to be available regularly and often to see the patient through to the end. It demands energy and faith in the one who gave himself for us so that through suffering and even death we might be his for time and eternity.

THE PASTOR'S RISK OF AIDS

What if the pastor gets AIDS in being with the AIDS patient? Wrong question! The pastor's visit to the AIDS patient is more a danger to the patient than the reverse, due to the patient's own lowered immunity. If the AIDS patient is threatening to the pastor's health, appropriate infection control measures should be taken by the pastor—such as a surgical mask if necessary and hand washing after a visit. The AIDS virus does not thrive outside the body for long and is easily destroyed by antimicrobial soaps.

During the Black Plague of the Middle Ages, the highest number of casualties proportional to the general population *were* not only doctors but also clergy—for obvious reasons. With the doctors, clergy were people called by God to care for the sick and dying. But unlike the Black Plague, AIDS is not an airborne disease and is not communicable by casual contact. Even if it were, could the church stop caring for those in need of God's healing, which lasts eternally? We give thanks for the opportunity to minister, in spite of the difficulties of relating to AIDS patients, and we reach out in love under the cross.

AIDS UNDER THE CROSS

AIDS under the shadow of the cross means that we have no temporal cure to offer, but rather an eternal grace by which God walks with sufferers through the valley of the shadow of death. The very sense of helplessness pastors feel (along with the calling they have to continue to reach out in love) demonstrates God's own predicament in loving us. Just as God does not abandon us either because of the difficulty in reaching us or the likelihood of our rejection, so we reach out pastorally to AIDS patients whenever God puts the challenge before us. Whatever may be done to provide assistance in the home or the hospital, pastoral care is the only hope that reconciles an AIDS patient to God and to those from whom he is alienated. Other disciplines may offer acceptance of the homosexual, but pastoral care helps the sufferer find healing for it. And healing begins with the need for faith—as it does with anyone else. In the context of faith, the homosexual has opportunity to see the meaning of sexuality as God intends it. Thus, the calling of pastoral care is a gift of God to AIDS patients.

On the Cross: Dying

Instruction in pastoral care of the dying and of those who mourn
will require separate chapters since the needs of each are different.
In this chapter we will consider providing pastoral care for the spiritual needs of the dying, but first we need to understand the current perception of death.

The terms our culture uses for death help us understand how it
is perceived. At two o'clock in the morning, an emergency room
nurse telephones me: "We have a pulseless nonbreather here; will
you come in?" To this strange description of what most of us would
call a dying person, I am tempted to reply, "What kind of a crea-
ture is it? What does it look like?" When a patient dies, hospitals
use a wide range of descriptive terms: from "expired" (the metaphor
of a subscription that ran out) to "fatal demise" to "a patient died."
Such disparity reflects the divorce of the clinical and the human, just
as it describes the uneasy alliance between medicine and religion
today. I recall my first experience of a doctor's announcing the news
of a death. A teenage couple had been out driving and drinking,
and there was an accident. The young girl survived, but her
boyfriend died. The doctor informed her of the fact by saying, "He
didn't live through it." Although he tried to soften death by avoidance of the word "died," her grief was the same.

THE CONTEMPORARY DENIAL OF DEATH

Applying Paul Tillich's description of ancient, medieval, and
modern anxieties, Peter Kreeft of Boston College says, "[T]he
ancient pre-Christian mind was death-accepting (and fatalistic); the
medieval Christian mind was death-defying (believing in the resurrection); and the modern post-Christian mind is death-denying
(looking away from death as a stranger)."[1] "For centuries," Kreeft
continues, "people prayed 'to be spared a sudden and unprovided

death.' They feared *not* thinking about death more than death itself. Today, people hope for a 'sudden and unprovided death' so that they might not have time to think about it. They fear *thinking* about death more than death itself!"[2]

The problem pastors face today is that people come face to face with death, increasingly unprepared by a post-Christian culture that postpones indefinitely any thoughts about death. Even Christians, while confessing "the resurrection of the body," often avoid thinking too much about death and fear the pastor's open discussion of the subject at the bedside.

In all my years as a hospital chaplain I recall only a few patients who on their own initiative talked openly of their spiritual needs in the face of death. (In nearly every case I initiated such conversations.) Bill, in his 30s, weighing over 300 pounds, and describing the substance of his life as "women, booze, and fast cars," asked to see a chaplain. As I entered the room, he was sitting on the edge of his bed, struggling to get his breath. Bill had lung cancer. After a few moments I asked, "What can I do for you, Bill?" His reply was clear: "I don't want to go to hell." Although rejecting the Christian faith most of his young life, he now wanted to "make his peace with God." Shortly before his death Bill said to his mother on the phone, "Mama, I believe; I believe." And on the day of his death, as she and I sat at his bedside, it was clear that Bill *did* believe and was prepared to die.

Another patient who clearly expressed a desire to speak about spiritual concerns in the face of death was a 45-year-old homosexual male with AIDS. He requested, "Help me find my way back to God." However, as time went on and death seemed less imminent, his interest in finding his way back to God waned.

Yet another patient, speaking openly but from disbelief, conveyed the modern, death-denying attitude clearly: "Don't waste your time with me. I appreciate your attention, but I don't believe in God, and I am sure there are others who need you more."

People today believe the way to face death bravely is to deny that it has any meaning at all. Strange as it sounds, for many, admitting that death is bad news is no longer easy. Unprepared to face death honestly and without the help of others who see death for what it is, people have no choice but to reject the reality of death altogether through denial. This explains why pastoral care must sometimes be confrontational as well as comforting. Even patients at the point of death often do not want to prepare to meet God and so spend their energies instead on denying their imminent deaths. One patient developed the most sophisticated avoidance technique I have ever seen. Each time I visited him, he begged me to help him get a date with the nurse caring for him.

DEATH AS NATURAL VERSES DEATH AS ENEMY

Although "the good news of Christianity claims to answer the bad news of death,"[3] many today choose to follow the ancient Greek philosopher Socrates, who claimed that death is something natural, a friend. In contrast, Jesus viewed death as an enemy to be feared. While Socrates seemed to die by his own hand with apparent peace of mind, Jesus, in the Garden of Gethsemane, resisted the prospect of dying and he sweat blood in his anxiety. He knew death was the wages of sin, the judgement of God. On the cross he even cried out, "My God, why have you forsaken me?"

In contrast, Dr. Elizabeth Kübler-Ross' book *Death and Dying* found a receptive market with its "how to" approach to the mastery of dying. As a modern-day Socrates, Kübler-Ross has persuaded our culture to see death as natural and even desirable rather than as "the wages of sin." Even Christians sometimes confuse this form of denial ("death as natural") with the Christian teaching that believes those who die are "asleep in Jesus",[4] awaiting Jesus' wake-up call on the Last Day. A realistic and therefore salvific view of death must first regard death as the enemy, and only after that regard it as sleep that has no power over those who are in Christ. For only death as the "wages of sin" and Jesus' Easter victory that conquers death provide any genuine peace and hope.

HUMAN NEEDS OF THE DYING

In order to overcome the denial of death, it is important to understand human needs and spiritual needs. In this section, we look at the human needs of the dying. All people, Christians and non-Christians alike, have some basic needs that emerge at the time of death, including the need to grieve our loss of life and the loved ones we will leave behind, the need to sum up life and discover meaning in its broad spectrum of experiences, and the need to do one's dying alone. If the dying person cannot admit these needs and face up to them, he will try to protect himself by denying that death is a threat.

Pastoral care helps the dying person face these human needs by pointing out the legitimacy of our human needs before God. Although Kübler-Ross may appear to point out human needs of the dying, it is based on the assumption that the way to gain control over fears is through understanding dynamics alone. I have never seen a dying patient comforted by this. Comfort comes from the message of pastoral care that makes the connection between human needs and God. This need for God leads the pastoral caregiver to address the spiritual needs of the dying.

Spiritual Needs of the Dying

The two most feared and therefore most avoided realities of life in our time are the realities of helplessness (or loss of control) and dependency. Our culture prizes self-determination as the highest good and views helplessness as the greatest threat. Our culture values autonomy as the first priority and labels dependence on others as "humiliating and dehumanizing." (In a later chapter we will see how this message leads to ethically questionable choices in medical care of the sick and dying.)

The Christian witness of each generation must speak to people's greatest fears. Therefore, pastoral care in our time must begin with people's fears of helplessness and dependency, fears that increase in the face of our own or someone else's terminal illness. As someone has said, "We are all terminally ill." A 51-year-old wife and mother, diagnosed with cancer, treated with chemotherapy, and discharged from the hospital all in less than one week, needs pastoral care. The fact that she seems to be coping does not mean she has begun to face her loss of control over life and her need to be cared for rather than to provide care for her family. Her mortality reminds her family and friends that they all live by grace. Their lives hang by a thread. Solution to this helplessness does not lie within ourselves but within God's care for each of us. A pastor reminds both the dying woman and those closest to her that being at God's mercy is a good place to be. This is the theology of the cross. In the midst of death we are in life. In the midst of our own helplessness, a Helper walks beside us who has gone the way of death before us.

Although it is true that people today may fear the helplessness and dependence of dying more than death itself, pastoral care must focus on preparation for eternity as well as on comfort in dying. The advantage of ministry to those who know they are soon to die is that their fears are too close to the surface to be displaced or dulled by superficial coping mechanisms. Helping them verbalize their fears, the pastor soon can encourage and support them in looking honestly at their relationship with God. And even though people may reflect culture's quick and easy belief in immortality-of-some-kind for all, we can accompany them through their "valley of the shadow of death" with all its threatening fears, pointing them to Jesus' death, which conquers both death and our justified fears. Doing this takes gentleness and careful timing. It is neither justified nor effective to attempt to frighten a person into faith. Rather, we must be "wise as serpents and innocent as doves." The pastor's ability to help a person look at his fears will begin with the pastor being comfortable with his own fears. People can sense whether the pastor is being honest with himself or whether he is only relying on technique alone to draw them out. If they feel he is honest, they will begin to speak of their own fears.

The Fear of Dying

Christians are not exempt from fears of dying. It is no more a lack of faith for a Christian to fear dying than it was for Jesus in Gethsemane to desire to live rather than to die. Christians also fear the suffering that may precede death. The beauty of Jesus' agony and bloody death is that he faced the worst of our fears and demonstrated that ultimately they are powerless. Rather than deny our fears and pretend that death is something natural, Christians can acknowledge their deepest fears and needs. Christians may become angry in the face of death, recognizing that it ought not be that way. Death was not God's intention when he created this world. Often dying people aim their anger at those around them or at themselves, but sometimes they direct their anger at God. Pastoral care should allow people to get angry at God. In fact, it is a goal of pastoral care to encourage complaint to God, even in the form of anger. To whom else can we go when really frustrated and frightened than to God? God can handle it.

Sometimes, rather than voice their fears and anger about dying, Christians hold their feelings inside where feelings turn into depression. Such depression ought not be equated with loss of faith. A pastor who regularly visits a depressed terminally-ill person and listens patiently can encourage the dying person to distinguish feelings from faith and to verbalize the feelings, assured that anger and fear do not erase his relationship with God.

When ministering to dying people who are frightened, angry, or depressed, the pastor's provision of the Lord's Supper feeds the faith of the dying in a way that human comfort cannot. In this eating and drinking God provides strength to walk through death's passage.

Theology of the Cross

Nowhere more than in ministry to the dying is it evident that the suffering and death of Jesus Christ are at the heart of pastoral care. Christians do not need to look to the death-denying culture to interpret death for them, but to the Lord himself, as he faces death on the cross for us. Jesus' dying is conveyed to us through Baptism. As Paul writes, "Do you not know that all of us who have been baptized into Christ Jesus were baptized into his death? We were buried with him by baptism into death, so that as Christ was raised from the dead by the glory of the Father, we too might walk in newness of life."[5] And, "Our old sinful self was crucified with him."[6] And again, "You have died and your life is hid with Christ in God."[7]

This connection between Baptism and Jesus' death is a critical one that Christians need to understand. Baptism is the sign of Christ's victory over death. But more than a sign, Baptism also conveys God's undeserved kindness (grace) to us; when we were still as helpless as infants, in our Baptism God incorporated us into his victory. When Christ died on the cross, we died with him. When he rose from the dead, he pulled the plug on the impact of death on us. He disconnected the power of death to harm us, making death a whimpering and defeated tyrant. The benefit of Christ's victory is poured over us in Baptism. Now throughout life, God calls us to live that victory by faith.

Pastoral care reminds people that the victory over death is already theirs; death cannot destroy Christ's people in hell. What is of real importance at the time of death is not the suffering that precedes death, but the eternal suffering after death, the result of people alienating themselves from God. Nor is it that we fear the unknown in death but, rather that at some deeper spiritual level we really do fear that which is known, namely death as the wages of sin.

Christ's death correctly interprets death: Death, our enemy, leaves us helpless and without self control. Death is the consequence of being part of a fallen world, where the underlying condition of alienation from God is so strong that it kills us. Living in a fallen world, it remains for Christians to face the limited power of death to kill the body but not the soul. By reminding the dying of their Baptisms, pastors remind them that they have only their physical dying to do before reaching fulfillment in eternity.

The Necessity of Dying Alone

Pastors should expect the dying to withdraw from loved ones as they prepare to die alone. First, a dying person commonly withdraws from the wide circle of friends and community, and the family takes on greater significance. As illness progresses, the dying will often look to a particular member of the family for care and eventually may respond only to that person. Families may not understand why a dying loved one will no longer speak to them, but once he or she has said all that needs to be said, it is no longer necessary or often possible to keep the communication going. The relationships of a lifetime come down to the one relationship that the dying person needs most, the relationship with God, whom the dying one finally faces alone.

The pastor is often companion to the dying along with family members. He provides spiritual comfort that helps the dying learn to be alone with God as the end draws near.

When my father was dying in the hospital, he said goodbye in his own way to the family. Thereafter, he focused attention on me as the one he believed who knew both medically and spiritually what he needed. Each evening I prayed with him and read to him from the Bible. His last words to me were, "Thank you for all you have done for me." I replied, "You would have done the same for me, Dad." He responded, "Yes, I would." We were at peace with each other. He had given me his blessing, and he began the last steps of his walk with God alone.

When temporary improvement or recovery delays death, knowing how to bring comfort in that situation may not be easy. That is often why friends often stop visiting. What we instinctively want to do or say may be the opposite of what is needed. The visitor who comes to bring a smile to the face of the dying creates a temporary distraction from death, but the one who invites openness to the reality of death in a nonthreatening way brings new life. The degree of openness a dying person can tolerate will vary with each person. The pastor's goal will be to help the dying person to "save face" as he tests the intimate waters of his dying. At no time is bluntness about death appropriate. Such bluntness assaults the dying.

Although friends of the terminally ill may eventually stop visiting (possibly because of their own discomfort), pastors bring a word from God and teach the dying how to speak with God about their dying. The ultimate goal of the pastor's relationship with the dying is to move the dying person into fellowship with God. Even when little can be said or done, ways to nurture faith remain all the way up to death's door.

On one occasion when I was at a loss for words, I found myself in song. A woman in Intensive Care was believed to be unresponsive. Unable to communicate in words, with touch, or by movement, she had been slowly dying as medical complications increased. Late one night as I stood by her bed, I prayed with her and then, almost without thinking, began to sing softly, "Jesus loves me, this I know; for the Bible tells me so. Little ones to him belong; they are weak, but he is strong." As I finished singing the chorus, a

104

single tear trickled from one of her closed eyes. She made no other response (if, indeed, this can be called a response), and she died a few hours later. Perhaps God spoke to her that night through a song that began as pastoral care and continued as part of a celebration by angels.

WHAT TO DO AT THE TIME OF DEATH

As death draws near, the pastor's presence is increasingly important. Sometimes dying people hold out until all family members have arrived from out of town, and then die shortly after. At some point it may be necessary to help the family give their loved one permission to die. (Some families, however, repeatedly "give permission" to a loved one to die even though the patient isn't ready to die. A person's death cannot be orchestrated to the family's convenience.)

If a dying person is alert and for a few moments alone, the pastor's offer of private confession and absolution may provide an appropriate release for the dying. Even those who may never have practiced private confession can be invited to regard it as a comforting last preparation. Holy Communion can follow as an assurance of grace and an invitation into eternity. As the moment of death approaches, some form of the "Commendation of the Dying" may be appropriate for both the dying person and the family. As a way to introduce the Commendation, the pastor might communicate the idea that we are now placing this dying person into the hands of a gracious God.

Family members who have suffered long in caring for the loved one may feel exhausted and relieved as death nears. They need to be told they have done well in bearing the burden they have. For example, each week for two years I visited one woman in her home as she cared for and tube-fed her comatose husband. At one point, standing across the bed from her as she again filled the syringe with nourishment, I said, "You're doing a good job." She looked up in surprise. "Thank you," she answered. "No one ever said that before. My friends tell me I'm foolish for doing this and that I should put him in a nursing home, but I want to do this." Pastoral care speaks approval from God. The pastor's words can be God's words.

Silence, however, may also be a comforting gift of God. At times, when all has been said, sitting with the family in a comfortable silence is appropriate. Small talk is not necessary, but prayer is good. Listening rather than speaking places the pastor into the circle of watchers with God's saints. Finally, when death has come, the pastor's gentle touch on the patient's head or hand in benediction completes his care of the dying.

Attention now turns to pastoral care of the mourners.

At the Foot of the Cross: Mourners

My father was 94 when he died after only two weeks of illness. On one level I am thankful for his long life, many healthy years, and the brief moments we had for prayer and Scripture together before he died. On another level, I mourn his death and continue to miss him. This feeling of loss is called grief. At his funeral a dear friend tried to comfort me by saying, "He will rise, and you will see him again." Although touched by this friend's well-intentioned attempt to comfort me, I replied perhaps a bit angrily, "Yes, I know, but right now I need to remain at the foot of the cross, and I am feeling the pain of his being taken from me." I spoke before I thought, but that is what was happening. I was just beginning to feel the pain of his death and his absence from my life for the first time in my 52 years. I didn't want that pain taken away from me too quickly. I was grieving for myself, and I needed to remain at the foot of the cross a while before moving slowly to the empty tomb for comfort, healing, and hope.

You simply can't hurry the healing that comes one, slow drop at a time during the weeks, months, and even years following a death. Pastors need to be sensitive to this slow process and neither rush nor abandon mourners once they appear to be functional again following the funeral. Psychologists who study the dynamics of grief say it takes a year or more for the average person to face the changes brought about by the death of a loved one. I have counseled elderly persons who have never recovered from the loss of their spouses.

As much as each of us mourns in his own way and in his own time, in some ways we all mourn the same way. In this chapter we will look at the things we share in common and at our common comfort of God's healing at the foot of the cross.

A COMMON MOURNING: MEN AND WOMEN

Sudden, sometimes dramatic deaths, those that occur because of automobile accidents, heart attacks, or while cutting the backyard lawn frequently bring mourners to a hospital emergency room where their grieving begins in earnest. A man finds his 47-year-old wife unconscious on the floor of their home and calls the paramedics, who bring her to the emergency room. There, she is worked on for nearly 45 minutes, but she never regains consciousness and is pronounced dead. Her husband, sitting in the nurse's office where he can have privacy, waits for news of his wife who he knows instinctively didn't make it. After several reports, he knows from the look in the nurse's eyes when she enters that his wife has died. He is alone with us, nurse and chaplain, and weeps quietly for a few moments, finally asking to see his wife. We visit her together, and he gently hovers over her, often caressing her body as if beginning to make love to her. He weeps silently and suddenly turns away. "What do I have to do now?" he asks. The papers are signed for an autopsy, the name of a funeral home given, and he receives her belongings in a bag and leaves.

If, however, a husband has died and the wife waits in the nurse's office, the scene might differ slightly. At each entrance of the nurse bringing an update, the wife greets her with wide-eyed hope of good news or tearful fears of the worst. Even in the face of reports preparing her for his death, she hopes for the best. Wives seem to wait hopefully, while husbands seem to fear the worst.

When word comes that her husband has died, the wife weeps profusely; and if others are present she is comforted with hugs and shared tears. When she is taken in to see her husband, she weeps aloud and may need physical support to stand at his bedside. Her grief is instant and deep. She is not concerned to make a good appearance. She will seek the comfort of others to share her pain. In the long run, however, in spite of her openness, others may think that she is taking an excessive time to grieve because she faces head-on every aspect of her loss. In contrast, a man appears to put it all aside and manage as best he can. In reality, the man, more than the woman, may be least prepared and least capable of grieving well.

Expected, awaited deaths often come as a relief after a long, wearying illness. When death occurs, the grieving usually begins slowly, even quietly, and sometimes takes a while to be felt as deeply as a sudden death. Many terminally-ill people die at home surrounded by those who care about and for them. Home hospices usually provide excellent care, and its caregivers frequently follow up for support after a death. It is a commendable system of care, but in a way sad for those of us who remember that it used to be the congregation who provided such care and comfort. But sometimes only the pastor calls as death draws near, and he alone may follow up for a week or two to comfort.

Pastors, as men, may have to pay special attention to what women of the congregation can provide instinctively, namely a support that is patient and that listens long to talk about a loved one. A woman of the congregation with a gift for this kind of support might be enlisted by the pastor for additional care of those mourning.

Following years or months of illness, those awaiting the inevitable death in a hospital are often relieved that it is over when death comes. Tears flow, but they are more likely controlled and deliberate. When family is present day after day, sitting at the bedside, awaiting the end, it is sometimes not immediately obvious that the end has come; so nurses are called in to verify the death. For those who await word in their homes or at work, support from family and friends is usually present. Calls are made in leisure, and the family leaves the hospital after discussions of the patient's long illness with the nurses. Grief seems to begin slowly and to become more intense as the days and weeks pass. It is a mistake for the pastor to think that the mourner's immediate calm exterior is anything more than a shroud of relief over the deeper hurt that has hardly begun to emerge. Relief, numbness, calm weeping, and gradual emergence of pain take their turn in surfacing.

THE PACE OF MOURNING

A study of widows shows some reactions and themes common to mourners in their bereavement.[1] At the time of death, feelings usually fluctuate between panic and complete numbness. Any pastor who has been present the moment a husband's death is announced to the wife has seen this paradox. Although the panic of tears is wrenching, it is the widow's numbness and emotional inaccessibility that is most disturbing for the pastor. It is as if this grieving person is deaf to all comfort, perhaps lost, deep in some other world. Real pain begins about 10 days after the death—when the funeral is over, everyone has left, and loneliness is felt for the first time. At this point a leisurely visit from the pastor is most helpful, because the widow (or widower) can finally talk about things and begin to hear the comfort that was all a blur during the funeral.

In the weeks following a death a mourner needs both to be alone and to experience the comfort of pastor and friends. Too often people stop visiting once the funeral is over. Because things get back to normal for everyone else whose life has been disrupted by these events, the mourner is often neglected. About a month later, for those making a good adjustment, hope dawns and life begins to take on worth again. At this point women (seldom men) have come to my office to talk about this change. Frequently, they express some guilt over beginning to feel good again, especially if others are inviting them to social engagements. Surprised because they feel like accepting these invitations, mourners need a friend's or pastor's permission to do so.

A difficult time of grieving occurs on holidays, anniversaries, birthdays, and on days that were special to the mourner and one who has died. These special events accentuate the loss and its consequences. Not until the grieving person has made it through a whole year without the loved one does he or she begin to think that perhaps life goes on after all.

Grief, felt deeply at first, gradually diminishes, only to be punctuated by moments of sometimes very intense pain as bereavement takes place. Sometimes grief returns for years at certain moments of remembrance. Mindful that grieving takes time, some congregations on one or several days throughout the year read the names of those who have died. Other churches note the anniversaries of deaths year after year. All such reminders of God's caring grace are beneficial and reinforce the truth that we are one body in Christ and individually members one of another.

Getting Stuck in Grieving

Like all crises in our lives, grieving provides an occasion for spiritual growth that the pastor ought not miss. But not all who grieve grieve well. While the pastor does not issue grades of pass or fail for grieving, he will do well to note how his parishioners are grieving and provide whatever support they need, especially if they get stuck in their grieving. Yet no mourner wants to be rushed, and it would be wrong to make everyone adhere to a schedule for grieving. Marriages that end after 53 years of life together require more time to grieve than does a year-old friendship. But even those who grieve a death under the easiest of circumstances can get stuck at some point in their grieving.

Most commonly, people get stuck at some point of anger. Such anger may not be apparent to others, especially if it takes the form of depression or a self-destructive behavior like in self-neglect or attempts at suicide.

Granger Westberg's classic, *Good Grief*,[2] notes that some people may become sick and need hospitalization if they are unable to handle their grief. In my hospital visits with patients who seem depressed and have many bodily complaints, I often inquire about events in their life over the past year or two. Not infrequently they will tell me that someone close to them, a son or daughter or spouse, for example, died about six months to a year-and-a-half ago (or longer for older people). These people say that at the time of the death they often felt little or nothing, being bewildered by it all. Although they are unable to accept the truth that the death has occurred at all, the grief clearly has remained inside them, eating away at body and soul. Encouragement to talk and patient listening often help. On occasion, counseling may be required once a week for a month or six weeks to resolve the conflict with the one who died or with the feelings of guilt and anger toward the deceased. In these situations, the church, through the pastor, can offer the medicine of forgiveness to heal the anger and guilt.

Mistaken piety that equates grief with lack of faith also may get in the way of completing the grief process. It is important to remember that Jesus wept at the announcement of Lazarus' death and probably would have continued to grieve if he had not raised Lazarus from the dead. Likewise, Paul writes, "[I would not have you] grieve as others do who have no hope."[3] Surely Paul is also saying, "Nevertheless, *do* grieve as those who *do* have hope." That is, grieve as caring for each other, knowing that someday we shall be together with the Lord. Only in the 20th century has mistaken piety prevented healthy tears from flowing, holding back the comfort others want to give. Until tears of relief can flow, grief will move slowly or not at all, and mourners will feel isolated and alone.

At the same time, it is important to note that some of the tears that flow freely are not tears of relief. Tears of anger ought not be misunderstood for tears of sadness. In counseling a man who had lost his wife, I noticed his eyes fill as he talked about her. Gently I asked him what his tears meant. A torrent of anger broke loose in which he blamed his wife for dying and leaving him with four young children. He went on to identify his anger at God for taking his wife away from him. As he spoke words of anger, his tears flowed and his grief, dammed up for months, flowed freely. The poison was running out of his soul. It did not take long before his tears of anger became tears of sorrow, and he begged God's forgiveness for the bitterness and resentment he had indulged for so long. In the midst of his grief, the man needed absolution. When the poison of his sin had been drained, the grace of forgiveness quickly healed him.

AT THE FOOT OF THE CROSS

When mourners kneel at the foot of the cross, they are inclined to look up to the one who saves them. At the cross mourners are compelled to look for comfort, not to those beside them who share their loss but up to Jesus. The main goal of pastoral care in the face of death is gently to direct all eyes to Christ for comfort and to help the mourners to love God more than the person who has died.

This is, of course, the aim of the Christian life at all times. We are to love God more than any human being. If we do not, then we have made an idol of husband or wife, son or daughter, lover or friend. Martin Luther warns us, "The soul may not and must not find contentment in any other thing but in the highest Good, which has made her and is the fountain of her life and blessedness. Therefore, God wills to be the One to whom the soul shall cleave and in whom she shall believe."[4] If the Christian wife gets stuck at some point in grieving her husband's death, the aim of pastoral care is to help her take her eyes off her husband and learn to love Jesus more than her husband.

This struggle over a divided loyalty is not easy to win. It requires a strong faith that is willing, gradually, perhaps, but finally to put her husband in God's hands and leave him there. Even the pastor's assurance that she will see her Christian husband again in heaven is not her primary hope, but secondary to the hope of seeing Christ. For all of us, Christ is the ultimate hope. Likewise, our hope of heaven does not focus ultimately on the promise of an afterlife but on being with the Lord. That is, we not only want to live again, but we want to be *with the Lord*. The hope of immortality is not unique to the Christian faith, but being with the Lord who made us, redeemed us, and now comforts us is. As Paul writes, "So we shall always be with the Lord. Therefore comfort one another with these words."[5]

Grieving at the foot of the cross reveals our situation. We have nothing to offer to remove our grief and nothing to hang on to but Jesus alone. Grieving teaches us to let go of everything we have had in the past and to live anew as God's grace allows. This does not mean that we have to let go of memories or that we have to stop talking about the past. Rather, we see the past in holy perspective, as God's gift of grace that continues to unfold in new ways until we are with the Lord in eternity. Letting go of the past is not disloyal to those who have died, as some mourners may think, but rather is an act of faith that entrusts to the Lord of life the completed and fulfilled lives of those who have died and of us as we await fulfillment in our own death. Our loved ones are with the same Lord who is with us. He unites saints on earth and in heaven into one family that shall be revealed when He returns.

The Pastor as Comforter

The tasks of the pastor are unique in the dying, death, and mourning of God's people. By Word and Sacrament the pastor brings hope to the dying, and at the time of a death he reminds the mourners how, in Baptism, God gave their loved one salvation. To comfort the mourners, the pastor feeds them with the same Word and Sacrament that sustained the deceased.

Others from the congregation also might be enlisted to assist those who mourn in making the physical and emotional adjustments necessary for a new life. Women especially seem to be good listeners, although a man speaking to another man in his sorrow is a treasured ministry the church ought to encourage. All such opportunities in the crises of faith we endure produce stronger faith and greater joy in the face of sorrow.

The pastor's presence (in addition to the representative laity of the congregation) following a death is important, because it is an opportunity for growth in faith. In addition to comfort, the mourners need to look at their life with the loved one and with God in honest and open ways. The wife who resented her husband, the husband who failed to appreciate his wife, and the children who neglected their parents need to find forgiveness as much as comfort for loss. When the time is appropriate and the bitterness is gone, a rite of individual confession and absolution offers healing for mourners. This is especially true when death has been due to suicide. The willingness to forgive and be forgiven is crucial to the healing of grief.

The pastor, in comforting the bereaved, needs to let mourners feel whatever they feel. Do not rush in to cure every wrong or hurt. Be patient, but know where you want to lead the mourner. Focus on the mourner, not on your need for the mourner to be where he or she can't yet be. Pray with the mourner, recalling things poured out in your presence. People look to their pastors in order to see Jesus. This is so important that some parishioners have left the church because their pastor never visited them following a death, and they felt abandoned by God as well. God does work through people, especially through those who bring God's healing grace in Word and Sacrament.

A CONCLUDING THOUGHT

I began this chapter with an account of my father's death. In the year following his death I found myself preoccupied with my mother's grief, with wearisome legal matters, and with the realiza-

114

tion that I too was growing older faster than I realized. I also have discovered a new outlook on some things in life since Dad's death. For one thing, I realize how much of what I did was done for Dad's approval. I also see how much I admired his abilities, some of which I have acquired. And I have learned how different it is not to be able to tell Dad things that he and I would have both enjoyed. But most of all, in my grieving I have learned to appreciate all that Dad gave me, both by his love and by his genes, and I have learned to put him back into God's hands each time I am tempted to feel sorry for myself at his loss. It is truly in looking up to Jesus that I have found comfort.

Crossing the Line: Mental Illness

UNDERSTANDING MENTAL HEALTH SPIRITUALLY

As Christians called to be "in the world but not of the world," we must understand mental illness in spiritual as well as psychological terms in order to recognize what we have to offer the mentally ill in the name of Jesus Christ. For most of this 20th century we have seen ourselves through the lens of psychology, which teaches that the only forces at work on us are the ones we create in our minds. We need to ask whether there isn't some reality at work beyond the mind.

The Christian is convinced that, although God interacts with people, an evil presence also exists as an entity apart from the human mind and gives evidence of "the devil and all his works and all his ways."[1] Martin Luther's "psychology" of the soul reminds us that "the old Adam in us should by daily contrition and repentance be drowned and die with all sins and evil desires, and that a new man should daily emerge and arise to live before God in righteousness and purity forever."[2] Almost from the beginning of time God's reign has been a disputed sovereignty, a conflict that engages us in spiritual warfare. Whether we say that people are inhabited by demons (as Jesus did), or we call them mentally ill, we are identifying a deeper reality in which sin and grace compete for the soul. Although few of us would be likely to reduce mental illness to demonology, our Lord surely is pointing us even today to the reality of the persona of evil and its spiritual powers, which have in mind to destroy the human soul.

The understanding of ourselves as psychological beings has been helpful in modern times, but it also has had its limitations.

We need to look beyond psychology to the deeper spiritual realities. What does it mean to be spiritual beings with spiritual problems for which God offers spiritual solutions? Pastors need to acknowledge and accept psychology, but at the same time recognize the ragged-edge limits of psychology as we reach out to the mentally ill to offer them the seamless robe of Christ.

I am not calling for the rejection of a psychological self-understanding or of the pharmacology that some pit against faith. Even if it were desirable, it would be impossible to shed our psychological perspective of ourselves. This perspective belongs to the spirit of the age in which we live and is daily reinforced in everything from advertising and the media to education and the workplace. Rather, we need to reintroduce to the world the deeper realities behind human thought and behavior. It may be that psychology will coincide with Christian truth in helping us uncover the individual's need for identity, community, stability, and the forgiveness of sins; but only Christ, through pastoral care, makes provision for these needs through the giving of himself on the cross. Good psychology recognizes its limitations and encourages the Christian to practice his or her faith and to be part of the healing faith community, the congregation. Likewise, faith does not replace the need for psychological counsel or for some medications, which often are gifts from God. The Christian need not pit faith against medicine per se. There is need, however, to come to a spiritual understanding of mental illness so that pastoral care can provide the healing God intends for those whose lives are a daily mental hell on earth.

For our purposes, therefore, we define mental illness theologically as every spiritually devastating effect of living in a disordered or fallen world in which some more than others experience a deeper loss of who and whose they are and find themselves cut off from the intimacy God provides, which orders our lives together. For all of us, spiritual health is found in knowing who and whose we are and in responding by faith accordingly.

A PASTOR'S SIMPLE GUIDE TO MENTAL ILLNESS

In order to minister more accurately to the needs of people, the pastor needs to understand the more common forms of mental illness. According to the DSM IIIR (the bible of psychiatry) some mental illnesses are organic and some are inorganic in origin. The more common mental illnesses fall into three categories: Schizophrenic Disorders, Anxiety Disorders, and Affective Disorders. These people are easy for the pastor to identify because of the excess to which their behavior witnesses. The Personality Disorders include Histrionic, Narcissistic, Avoidant, Dependent, Obsessive Compulsive, Passive Aggressive, and Borderline.

Schizophrenic Disorders

People with schizophrenia, when not receiving proper medications, are generally characterized by excessive thought disturbance, delusions, hallucinations, and bizarre behavior. Daniel, a 31-year-old man with Schizophrenic Disorder, came to my office asking to be exorcised of a demon. When I hesitated, he assumed I did not believe that he was demon possessed and demonstrated the demon's presence by growling and snarling. His excessive weight of more than 300 pounds gave his sound effects credibility. Between his subsequent visits I discovered through area pastors that Daniel had been around for a while and was known by them. Daniel, although legally residing with his mother, was one of the many street people who often came to the pastor for help. His schizophrenia was enhanced by periodic conflicts with his mother, with whom he generally lived. It may have been that Daniel was "possessed" by his mother more than by his demon.

Although people may suffer varying degrees of severity with schizophrenia, few of them are likely to be active, long-term members of a congregation, since their bizarre behavior is recognizable by others as "crazy." People with this disorder usually keep to themselves and do not make relational commitments at any intimate level.

How can a pastor be helpful? Perhaps setting limits of love, which are similar to what is known as "tough love" in substance-abuse circles, may be all that can be done. For the sake of both the pastor and the mentally ill person, a limit on time, attention, and frequency of contact allows for moments of caring without exhausting the pastor's personal resources.

Anxiety Disorders

More common among mentally ill people are those suffering Anxiety Disorders. For example, a person joins the church but can't tolerate people and stays only for the worship service. He sneaks in early or late, unseen, and sits in the balcony alone. People with Anxiety Disorders may suffer panic attacks, may have a sense of impending doom, may hold excessive and unrealistic fears, or may engage in obsessive compulsive behavior (such as excessive perfectionism) that interferes with daily living. While any of us may have some or many similar traits, it is their excessive and immobilizing nature that defines them as mental illness.

Affective Disorders

Among the Affective (mood) Disorders, Major Depression is most common. People with manic-depressive illness alternately show wide mood swings in which the person is excessively manic (euphoric, elated) and depressed. These disorders deserve much attention and will be dealt with at length in the next chapter.

Personality Disorders

Personality disorders do not appear to result from biological causes (although they can certainly have complicating biological problems), but result from very early life experiences. They tend not to be treatable with medications. (They may be a hereditary.) Women with Borderline Personality, because of their poor mothering skills, tend to raise children with personality problems. However, this is probably more a problem of nurture than of nature.

Differing from people with more common mental illness (Schizophrenia, Anxiety, and Affective Disorders), those who suffer from one of the dozen or so personality disorders are characterized by permanent, inflexible, maladaptive, and socially impairing personality traits. These people are more likely than those in the former category to be part of congregational life—and to cause heartache for the pastor, though it may not be obvious to others that they are mentally ill. Even though pastors are not mental health professionals, pastors need to be aware of the following disorders in order to

119

identify the spiritual needs in each of them: Histrionic, Narcissistic, Avoidant, Dependent, Obsessive Compulsive, Passive Aggressive, and Borderline. Personality disorders develop early in life, often appearing during teenage years, and are common in the general population in varying degrees. The Narcissistic Personality Disorder seems to be on the rise in recent years. How much our culture and current disfunctional family environment play into this development is an interesting speculation.

HISTRIONIC PERSONALITY DISORDER

People with the Histrionic (or Hysterical) Personality Disorder are characterized by excessive excitability and over dramatization. They "pole-vault over mouse dung" that everyone else seems to take in stride. Further symptoms include attention seeking and excessive need for approval by others. They often respond positively to authority figures such as the pastor, expecting them magically to solve their problems. They adopt strong emotional convictions in matters such as faith, but these convictions lack depth of insight. The pastor needs to recognize that these enthusiastic people will do anything for him so long as it enhances their ego and they get the praise they crave. His challenge is to provide appropriate approval while, again, setting limits on demands for more.

NARCISSISTIC PERSONALITY DISORDER

With an inflated sense of self-importance, people with a Narcissistic Personality Disorder expect everyone eise to give way to them. They lack empathy for others. For example, they might become angry with you for missing a luncheon appointment, even if the reason was a death in your family. Actually their self-esteem is fragile, and they seek reinforcement in order to know they are acceptable. Their need for acceptance, however, is a bottomless pit that is seldom satisfied. They react to any criticism with rage; they exploit others and believe they are entitled to that which others are not. Narcissism is one of the predominant characteristics of our culture at this time, sometimes emerging in public issues as a matter of "rights."

AVOIDANT PERSONALITY DISORDER

People with Avoidant Personality Disorder do not present a problem for the pastor as much as they do for themselves. They are uncomfortable in social settings and avoid them, usually making excuses for their absence because they fear that others will react negatively to them. Easily hurt, timid, and without close friends, these people truly are the lost sheep of any congregation. They need to know that God accepts them and that they are members of the body of Christ. People with Avoidant Personality Disorder (or any other disorder) do not change but have to be helped to live with their illness. The pastor may find that his contact with these people is the only contact they allow from the church.

DEPENDENT PERSONALITY DISORDER

Although loyal to the pastor, a person with a Dependent Personality Disorder is indecisive and has difficulty initiating projects. She will volunteer to do unpleasant or demeaning jobs in order to be liked by others and externally will agree with the pastor and with others even when there's no true agreement. Because the Dependent Personality type is common, parish pastors may look to dependent types to find willing volunteers who won't cause much trouble. But, as for all personality disorders, the pastor's objective is not only to make his own life more pleasant but to minister to their spiritual needs. The pastor must be careful not to overburden mentally ill yet eager volunteers, assuring them of God's gracious approval apart from works.

OBSESSIVE COMPULSIVE PERSONALITY DISORDER

Obsessive Compulsive people are perfectionists to the extreme: inflexible, resisting authority, and demanding that it be done "my way." Usually very bright people, they are immobilized by the fear of making the wrong decisions or of making mistakes. Because they are conscientious and moralistic, they judge themselves and others harshly. They are cold, aloof people, without much generosity of spirit. While they make good accountants or congregational treasurers, they tend to be unreasonable, controlling, and insensitive to the needs of others. The pastor will have to be firm in setting the parameters within which this kind of person is allowed to function in a position of authority in the congregation.

PASSIVE AGGRESSIVE PERSONALITY DISORDER

Among the most difficult personalities in parish life are those with a Passive Aggressive Personality Disorder. These people passively resist anything that does not originate with them. They are angry, sulky, irritable, argumentative, and aggressive people, yet they always appear "nice" to others. Their resistance comes through procrastination, dawdling, stubbornness, intentional inefficiency, and "forgetfulness." They obstruct the efforts of others by failing to do their share of the work.

Every congregation has its share of people with Passive Aggressive Personality Disorder who would neither recognize nor admit to their nature. If you pointed out to them their behavior, they would call you paranoid or unfair, because they're "only trying to do their best." In times of conflict with this kind of person, the pastor is advised not to explain himself, because the person will most likely distort any explanation and use it as ammunition against the pastor.

BORDERLINE PERSONALITY DISORDER

Equally difficult in parish life are people with a Borderline Personality Disorder. They suffer from identity disturbance; that is, they have no identity of their own and, without realizing it, take on the identity of others. They can be persuasive and charming, but also unstable, manipulative, and impulsive in destructive ways. They vacillate between inappropriate, intense anger and feelings of boredom and emptiness. Borderline people attach themselves to the pastor or another authority figure, approving everything he thinks, but turning on him in a moment if he intentionally or inadvertently says something they interpret as a sign of rejection or disapproval. These people are alarming for their adoration one day and their condemnation the next. The pastor is unwise to try to please such people. Rather, early in the relationship, he should set limits to their clinging

122

to him.

(Although pastors may be tempted to form close friendships with Borderline Personality parishioners, pastors generally should look outside the congregation among peers and those not under their pastoral care. Every pastor needs a life outside the congregation as well as within it.)

MENTAL ILLNESS AND THE THEOLOGY OF THE CROSS IN ACTION

The task of the church is not to cure mental illness but to address the legitimate spiritual needs of suffering people. If Luther's term *theology of the cross* means anything, it means that God chooses to come to people through suffering. Mental illness is one kind of suffering through which God draws near to people.

Penny, with a multiple, complex psychiatric diagnosis, spent six months in our psychiatric unit. She had had no religious background, and the nurses warned that she was psychotic (that is, in her own little world). Penny was truly "crazy." Nothing she said or did made any sense. When I visited her, she was inappropriate in her responses to me in everything except spiritual matters. In the midst of her craziness I was able to introduce Penny to God's grace, mercy, and love. Although she made several suicide attempts while in the unit (once even drinking the Lysol off the custodian's cart), she was always receptive to my visits and seemed to be listening behind the craziness. When she was placed in isolation for long periods of time, I visited with her (under-lock-and-key), read psalms to her, and talked of God's love. She always stopped her craziness long enough to listen.

Toward the close of her six-month stay, Penny began to improve from a psychiatric point of view. At the same time she deteriorated spiritually. I was stunned that her spiritual responses, so appropriate when she was ill, deteriorated as she got well. Before she was discharged from the hospital, I wrote down for her the name of a congregation near her home.

A year later, we ran into each other in a shopping mall, and she related that she had been doing well and had joined that congregation, giving evidence of a genuine, healthy faith. I have no idea what all went on in my ministry to Penny at this terrible time in her life, but she continues to do well several years later, and I conclude that in her weakness and helplessness God helped her to see himself in the midst of it all as her Savior.

Ministry to mentally ill people requires that we stand out of the way of God's care. We must also learn to set limits, so that we do not do people an injustice by providing them an opportunity to act out their illness on us. We must offer evidences of God's caring, both through the limits we set on our relationship with them and also through our presence. At the same time, we must carefully assess whether we are inappropriately or unconsciously asking them to meet our own unhealthy needs to be liked or loved. Even pastors have personality disorders that feed on others.

If much of mental illness can be characterized by a loss of identity, community, and stability resulting in the absence of intimacy with God and other people, then surely pastoral care must seek to provide what the church has to offer to secure these life essentials. Identity as a baptized child of God; community within the Body of Christ; stability based on our eternal hope in Christ; intimacy with God based on Jesus' Incarnation ("God with us")—these are the medicine we pastors bring. Mentally ill people are often receptive to these, since at the root of their lives they crave what God desires to give. Ministry to the mentally ill is distressing, requiring long-suffering patience and wisdom, but it is also an exciting challenge that God gives to us who come in his name "as called and ordained servants of the Lord."

Some years ago a psychiatrist asked me to be a counseling resource to his Christian patients. Himself an orthodox Jew, he believed in the importance of spiritual as well as psychological resources for his patients. I accepted and began working in some depth with his Christian clients. Subsequently, he and I taught a course for second-year psychiatric residents at the Medical College of Wisconsin. I was impressed by the eagerness with which those residents wanted to learn about the normal beliefs of the Christian faith so that they could distinguish them from those perverse expressions of Christianity that frequently show up in mental illness. What also struck me was the loss of spiritual counsel available to people in hospital psychiatric units when their pastors play therapist instead of being pastors.

Although I must admit a certain fascination with psychiatry, I also have become increasingly aware of the importance and effect of spiritual care of the mentally ill. Pastors need to think creatively of ways to convey the love of God in Christ through Word and Sacrament.

In the next chapter I will avoid attention to psychology until the end, in favor of spiritual care of the mentally ill. Perhaps by telling what I have done pastorally, I can inspire other pastors to offer full spiritual care.

Feeling Crossed Out: Depression

DEPRESSION AND PASTORAL CARE

Claudia: The Too Small Self

Claudia, a simple, uneducated, single, 42-year-old woman, could be considered slow or marginally retarded. Employed for nearly 20 years as a live-in housekeeper, she was expected also to care for her employer's invalid wife. Claudia managed to keep her job as housekeeper-caregiver because of her imagined love affair with her employer, the invalid's husband.

Although the love was imagined, the sexual contact was not. For much of those 20 years she was sexually exploited. The husband had promised that when his wife eventually died, he would marry Claudia. However when his wife died, he dismissed Claudia as housekeeper, caregiver, and lover. Shortly thereafter, she ended up as a patient in our hospital's psychiatric unit with the diagnosis of depression, due mostly to her guilt over the years of sexual intimacy with the husband-employer.

I met Claudia when a nurse suggested I see her because nothing seemed to be helping Claudia pull out of her depression. Claudia accepted my invitation to visit with her, and I discovered that she was Lutheran and had been confirmed as a teenager. She talked about her confirmation instruction and recalled the words "Thou shalt not commit adultery." Angry at having been "used," Claudia also knew that she had done wrong. She was burdened with guilt, finding it hard to believe God would forgive her.

After listening to Claudia's confession, I visually described to her the struggle raging inside her between her sinful self and her forgiven self, reflecting Luther's *simul justus et peccator* (the idea that Christians are "sinners and saints at the same time"). I said, "You're depressed because you feel extreme guilt and can't believe God will forgive you. You can see the sinful life, but the forgiven life is too small to see. We need to feed your forgiven self so it grows big enough for you to see and believe. Therefore, I will bring Communion to you each day when we visit, and it will feed your forgiven self so that it grows bigger." It was a simple visual aid, illustrating the profound truth that God nourishes and feeds the crushed and broken sinner.

Claudia accepted my offer, and for the next three weeks we talked and prayed, and daily she received Communion. Her progress was remarkable. Not only did she recover from her depression (in part due to having also been given antidepressants), but she gained a whole new sense of self-worth and meaning to her life. Although never in her life had she lived on her own, upon her discharge from the hospital she found an apartment and also joined a Lutheran congregation. A year later I heard that she was still doing well. Her forgiven self had taken hold, and she was continuing to grow in Christ. Claudia is evidence of Paul's words, "We are hard pressed on every side, but not crushed; perplexed, but not in despair; persecuted, but not abandoned; struck down, but not destroyed."[1]

A House Swept Clean of Depression

Jesus' parable gives us another way to understand depression spiritually.

> When an evil spirit comes out of a man, it goes through arid places seeking rest and does not find it. Then it says, "I will return to the house I left." When it arrives, it finds the house swept clean and put in order. Then it goes and takes seven other spirits more wicked than itself, and they go in and live there. And the final condition of that man is worse than the first."[2]

While I do not want to suggest that depression is the equivalent of demon possession, Jesus' words nevertheless warn us that in a sinful world the person who does not know God may be able for a while to cope with many things (including depression) but cannot find ultimate meaning and hope in life without God. Hope born of trust in God must fill the void of our lives or else something destructive will. Louis' story illustrates this.

Louis came to his doctor for help in fighting what was soon diagnosed as a mild depression. After a few weeks on antidepressants, Louis did not feel any better. In fact, he felt worse and had begun to think suicidal thoughts, which frightened him. Louis was hospitalized for his safety and to allow him to better control his depression. Louis' antidepressants were changed several times, but still he showed little sign of improvement. Finally, after several electroconvulsive treatments, he showed signs of improvement and was released from the hospital. Louis agreed to see the psychiatrist monthly and to attend a psychotherapy group weekly. A cure seemed to have been effected, but a few months later he suffered some personal losses, his depression returned, and he was hospitalized a second time. "This time," Louis said to me, "I will never get well." In Jesus' words the "last condition of the man is worse than the first."

Clinically, what was happening to Louis? Filled with overwhelming anxiety, he sought a counselor. A good listener, the counselor helped Louis vent his anxiety, and Louis felt relieved when the session was over. But after the initial relief of identifying and expressing his feelings of anxiety, Louis did nothing more, his anxiety began to return, and he realized there was still something missing. More was needed than momentarily getting rid of something negative. Something or Someone was needed to fill the void in Louis' life and help him face his problems. The point of Jesus' parable is that only God can rightly fill the void of our lives.

This illustration does not mean to say that being a Christian will necessarily prevent depression. Rather, Jesus gives meaning and purpose to life, and he walks with us through depression. He knows our feelings of depression from his Gethsemane experience and from his feelings of abandonment by God on the cross.

As a crucial ingredient in ministry to the depressed, the pastor needs to understand the distinction between feelings and faith. They are not the same thing: Subjective feelings are not the objective promise God gives to us that he will never forsake us. This presence of Christ is fulfilled—dramatically for the depressed—in physical form by Christ's body and blood in the bread and wine of Communion and also in the presence of the pastor who gathers with the depressed person in Christ's name. Psychiatry may "sweep and put the house in order"; but to make it a home, an empty house needs the new furniture of hope which Christ offers and a family of support where two or three gather together in his name.

New Furniture

Father John, a retired Roman Catholic priest and a recovering alcoholic, had been dry for two years when he was admitted to the hospital for depression. One day as I entered the long corridor of the psychiatric unit, John was just coming out of his room at the other end. Seeing me, he plodded slowly toward me, until he finally stood speechless before me. He seemed to be searching for something inside me when he asked, "Is there any hope?" I replied, "Yes, John, there is hope in our Lord." He nodded, turned and walked back to his room. Our visit was ended, because John had heard what he needed to hear from me.

Hope, both the promise and the reality of it, is the new furniture that needs to fill the depressed person's empty house once psychiatry has swept it clean. Pastoral care is in the business of providing that new furniture.

Hope is not a feeling or even a wish for things to be different but a present reality based on the promises of God. Hope in Christ can offer relief from depression, but it also offers meaning and purpose in an otherwise pointless existence. John's need for assurance grew out of more than the need for relief from feelings. He needed to know there was more to life than he was feeling at the moment and that feelings are not the measure of faith. C. S. Lewis wrote to a friend elated with his new-found faith,

> It is quite right that you should feel that 'something terrific' has happened to you... Accept these sensations with thankfulness as birthday cards from God, but remember that they are only greetings, not the real gift. I mean that it is not the sensations that are the real thing. The real thing is the gift of the Holy Spirit which can't usually be ... perhaps not ever ... experienced as a sensation or emotion. The sensations are merely the response of your nervous system. Don't depend on them. Otherwise when they go and

you are once more emotionally flat (as you certainly will be quite soon) you might think that the real thing had gone too. But it won't. It will be there when you can't feel it. May even be most operative when you can feel it least.[3]

The house swept clean of depression needs the new furniture of hope, and pastoral care delivers it direct from the cross, assuring us that God is with us in the midst of suffering and makes himself known as our salvation in this life's depressions as well as in eternal life's joys.

A FAMILY OF SUPPORT

In addition to the new furniture of hope, a house swept clean of depression also needs a family of support to live there. Robin had been hospitalized for depression so many times that the nursing staff groaned when they heard she was being readmitted. Robin's behavior on the unit was not particularly difficult to manage, but any real success in moving her beyond frequent recurrences of depression had proven unsuccessful.

Robin responded to my visits without enthusiasm, but at least she was willing to accept them and to see me as one who brought God into her drab life. After her depression lifted and she was preparing to leave, I arranged for her to telephone me once a week to let me know how she was doing. We also agreed to enlarge her family of support beyond my spiritual care to include a local congregation. I called a pastor near her home and asked if he could find some volunteer work for her to do in the church among caring people. Eager to be of help, he created work for her to do in the office, where she would be with several others. Shortly after that Robin began attending worship services.

In the past, several things had made Robin's hopes of overcoming her destructive lifestyle and depression rather bleak. For one thing, she was the target of her family's frustration and hostility whenever they needed to lash out against life. If her sisters were having marital problems, they would take it out on Robin. If her parents got drunk, they would single out Robin for abuse. Robin's old associates on the street only darkened this already dismal picture. Everyone she knew was equally damaged by violence and abuse, and she could not expect any healing to come from them. Robin needed a new family, a family of spiritual support, while continuing to live with her family of origin. Jesus included people like Robin in his prayer, "My prayer is not that you take them out of the world but that you protect them from the evil one."[4]

Following Robin's discharge from the hospital, she and I talked on the phone every week for nearly six months. Sometimes, when she was feeling suicidal, Robin would call several times a week. After two-and-a-half years and a gradual decline in calls, Robin no longer made contact but agreed to do so if she needed help. Her pastor continued to keep me informed, assuring me that she was doing well, since she had found the family of spiritual support she needed, first in me and then in the congregation.

I use the analogy of the house cleaning described by Jesus as a way to visualize pastoral care of the depressed. The pastor will support the need for *a clean sweep* (medical attention and counseling), the need for *new furniture* (hope) and the need for *a family of support* (the congregation).

Depression and Suicide

Robin's case raises the question of how to understand and respond to a depressed person's threats of or attempts at suicide. From time to time patients admitted to the psychiatric unit will tell me the only reason they did not attempt suicide is because they believed it was wrong in God's eyes. One patient made his fears clear: "If I take my own life, I will go to hell." I always affirm this possibility. In this instance a moral judgement can serve as preventive pastoral medicine. Those who make suicidal gestures are playing with eternal fire. I remind them, "'You are not your own; you were bought at a price.'[5] Suicide is wrong, and you might cut yourself off from the one hope you have."

I have also said to patients, "I want you to promise me that you will not attempt suicide." Often they can keep this promise because one person cares enough to want to prevent it. I usually supplement this prohibition with a request: "If you feel suicidal, call me." Making these promises builds a bond (if not a temporary dependency) that gets the suicidal person outside herself. It is especially necessary for the family of support to continue to care for a depressed person after a suicide attempt.

The family of faith, the person's congregation, needs to affirm the same two points. The people must communicate disapproval for the attempt at suicide, but they also should lavish words of love and forgiveness where there is contrition. When the depressed feel God is silent to their cry for help to such a degree that it leads to an attempt at suicide, the voice of God can again be heard in those who help the depressed rebuild their lives. Part of the rebuilding of lives speaks moral judgement against suicide, but part of it reaches out in love and support no matter how many times attempts are made.

Depression and Guilt

Although not all depression is traceable to guilt (as in Claudia's case) and although some depression seems to have organic origins unrelated to life's circumstances, all pastoral care of depressed people acknowledges sin and grace, and it attempts to offer hope and new life to those who feel they are living in the shadow of death. Likewise, pastoral care acknowledges that we are all sinners living in a broken and fallen world, and that we are the creators collectively of this fallenness and must bear responsibility individually before God for our part in the brokenness.

Depressed people often have a free-floating sense of guilt that they cannot relate to any cause for it. Generalized guilt is distorted and blown out of proportion in relationship to the trivia they identify as its source. It is unwise for a pastor to take confession of trivia seriously in this case—even less wise to offer absolution for particular trivia. The offer of absolution will not alleviate the guilt, and the person will feel even more discouraged. What the depressed person needs here, more than absolution, is the assurance of God's promise never to leave nor forsake him.

Depression and Faith

Depressed parishioners nearly always feel they have lost their faith; they doubt that God cares about them or that there even is a

God. Because people frequently equate their faith with their feelings, they conclude that, having lost their good feelings for God, they have also lost God. They need assurance of God's care rather than prodding to have more faith. Both a pastor's words and his presence embody God's caring. Regular and frequent visits by the pastor (his identity as pastor speaks as loud as his personal caring) are important. In the pastor's visit the depressed come face to face with the visual reminder that God has not forgotten them. I have even said to some, "I know you feel God has forsaken you, but I am here as a sign of God's care for you." As said earlier, the pastor's presence is God's promise fulfilled that God will "never leave you nor forsake you." We who are not depressed need to bear the burden of those who are and help carry them through the valley of this shadow of death.

KINDS AND SIGNS OF DEPRESSION

While pastors and other spiritual caregivers need to think pastorally and theologically about depression and other mental illnesses, it is equally important for them to learn the human side of identifying the kinds and signs of depression. We should not play amateur psychiatrist, but in order to be helpful to the depressed, a little knowledge is a good thing.

Depression—something that interferes with daily living—falls under the clinical diagnosis of Mood Disorders. Mood Disorders include both Depressive Disorders (feelings of depression only) and Bipolar Disorders (feelings of both depression and elation). Depressive Disorders are those long-term episodes of depression lasting months with no relief. Bipolar Disorders, on the other hand, are characterized by mood swings between the two poles of depression and elation. The symptoms of a high or manic period of a Bipolar Disorder include inflated self-esteem, decreased need for sleep, rapid flight of ideas, excessive activity, and the inability to pace one's activities. The manic parishioner volunteers for everything and never wants to say no. A Manic Personality person in the congregation is excessively and overly religious, intrusive and domineering, disorganized, and has a bizarre quality.

A major Depressive Disorder, on the other hand, is expressed as a loss of pleasure or interest in all or almost all activities. Common signs of depression include an empty feeling, ongoing sadness or anxiety, tiredness and lack of energy, sleep problems and early morning wakening, problems of eating and weight gain or loss, frequent crying, difficulty in concentrating, forgetfulness, feelings that the future looks grim and hopeless, and thoughts of suicide. Unlike a normal person who might have one or more of these, the person with a major depression has virtually all of these symptoms.

Everyone has periods (hours or a day) of feeling a little elated or a little depressed. These feelings are associated with appropriate reasons for excitement or sadness—for example, getting ready for a wedding (elation) or losing a loved one (depression). However, normal depression, sustained because of a difficult situation, can sometimes evolve into a major depression. It is important for the pastor to recognize Depressive and Bipolar Disorders and to refer a manic or depressed parishioner for psychiatric help.

Severely depressed people cannot be talked or counselled out of depression. As one psychiatrist said, "Insight-oriented psychotherapy for the depressed is like adding insight to injury." The severely depressed must be directed to get help, since they will not do so on their own. Someone must take charge, preferably a family member, who orders the depressed against all protests to see a doctor. Expressing sympathy to a depressed person only adds to depression. Directed caring is necessary; empathy is counterproductive. Depression should be understood as a problem within a limited time frame, with beginning and end, within which the pastor walks with the person through his emptiness to help him visualize God's presence. The pastor does well to do this while the person is also under the psychiatrist's care.

THEOLOGY OF THE CROSS AND DEPRESSION

From a spiritual point of view, depressed people are closer to feeling the reality of a fallen world than non-depressed people are. Isaiah expresses the feeling level of the depressed parishioner, "Truly, thou art a God who hidest thyself."[6] In a major depression a person is a victim, not a willing participant, in his own depression. At the same time, a suicide attempt needs to be met with disapproval, not sympathy; with forgiveness, not mere tolerance. While it is always important to hold depressed people accountable for their behavior, it is not appropriate to hold them accountable for their feelings of depression.

During depression a parishioner has opportunity to experience grace in the midst of complete helplessness as part of the theology of the cross. Luther says, "It is certain that man must utterly despair of his own ability before he is prepared to receive the grace of Christ."[7] I have always found depressed people to be receptive to grace. Grace is the commodity that the church needs to make evident through the pastor's willingness to bear with them while also helping them recognize, objectively, that God cares for them. The pastor's task is that of standing at the foot of the cross with the depressed parishioner as God raises that parishioner to life again.

At the Crossroad: Medical Ethics

After being in Intensive Care for several weeks, Maggie was moved to Intermediate Care. At 54, she had been close to death many times during her hospitalization and now, for the first time, seemed stable. All of her medical complications had been resolved except one: Maggie was unable to be weaned from the ventilator that supported her breathing. Unable to speak, but alert and content, she communicated by writing and by mouthing words clearly enough to be lip-read. Her communication and clarity of thought were good, but Maggie would be dependent on her ventilator for the rest of her life.

Surprisingly, Maggie was not devastated by this news; she was just glad to be alive. Her physician, however, was not satisfied with this result of his medical efforts and introduced to Maggie the idea of choosing death over life. Because Maggie and I had developed a pastoral relationship during her ordeal, her doctor one day asked me to have a final prayer with Maggie before he turned off her ventilator to "allow her to die."

I was surprised by this sudden decision and asked if Maggie had taken a turn for the worse. He replied that she had not, but that he had approached her with the option of choosing to die. Still surprised by this viable woman's decision to end her life, I asked how it came about. Her doctor told me that he had gotten her into this "mess" and it was his job to get her out. He then went on to say that he had approached her four times in the past week about her situation, and although she had given a clear no three times to his suggestion to end her life, on his fourth attempt he told her that she "would never get off the ventilator, that this is no way to live, and that it is costing the hospital and society a lot of money to care for her." He then added, "She turned her head to the side, and I took this to be a nod of yes."

136

During the night, as she slept, he had begun to turn down her ventilator. Now he was asking me to pray with her before he turned it off completely. Actually, he was asking me to give my blessing to his decision to end her life.

I refused. But in disagreeing with his decision, I tried to minister to him as much as to Maggie. In as loving a way as I could I observed, "This is wrong. You can't do this." Our calm, but animated discussion lasted a half hour in the hallway with passing nurses obviously upset with my disagreement. When the doctor could not be persuaded to reconsider, I said, "I think you are doing wrong, but if you do it I will also be here for you when you realize what you have done." Since he had already turned down the ventilator to the point of causing Maggie to be unconscious, I did not pray at Maggie's bedside but alone in my office.

UNDERSTANDING THE TIMES

Individualism

It is important to understand the times in which our present medical ethical dilemmas unfold. For generations we have been moving away from the physical-spiritual-moral integration produced by Christianity to the increasingly narrow perceptions of individualism, relativism, and utilitarianism of the modern era.

Individual accountability before God and responsibility to the neighbor—legitimate aspects of the Christian life—have been replaced by individualism. Like all "isms," individualism makes individual accountability and responsibility a false god. Individual*ism* is legitimate individuality turned into self-centeredness and self-interest. In current discussions of medical ethics the language of "patient's rights" and "the right to choose" subjectivizes all moral criteria.

Relativism

Furthermore, relativism, a reaction against moral certainty, argues there is no objective moral good. Each person creates his own meaning in life. Life becomes meaningful, not in what we choose, but by virtue of the act of choosing in itself. But instead of resulting in a meaningful life, the result is moral chaos. Hence, the current state of medical ethics.

Utilitarianism

Filling the void created by relativism, utilitarianism is the most pervasive ethical virus of all. Usefulness, the attitude that "if it works, do it," has become the primary guide for making decisions. Utilitarianism is not concerned with moral character or consequences. Whatever works, works. If utility is lost through illness or aging, life no longer has worth. The implications for medical-ethical decision making are self-evident—as illustrated in the case of Maggie. In the doctor's eyes Maggie's uselessness (and therefore, worthlessness) to herself and to society eliminated any reason for her to go on living.

The Hippocratic Oath

The growth of individualism, relativism, and utilitarianism has diminished loyalty to the Hippocratic Oath, to which doctors have sworn allegiance for nearly 2,400 years. Since the mid-1970s fewer medical schools have required students to accept the Oath. Furthermore, the 1973 Supreme Court decision on abortion made mockery of the words:

> I will use treatment to help the sick according to my ability and judgement, but never with a view to injury or wrongdoing. Neither will I administer a poison to anybody when asked to do so [euthanasia], nor will I suggest such a course. Similarly, I will not give a woman a pessary to cause abortion."[1]

Even these medical schools that continue to use the Oath are deleting these prohibitions against killing. However, it is my growing sense that some younger doctors are uneasy with these deletions. In speaking to 22 first-year medical students at a seminar on medicine and religion, I sensed their moral indignation on realizing that the profession of medicine had succumbed to the spirit of the age and had stepped aside from the mainstream of medicine.

It is incumbent on the pastor to understand the dynamics of ethical decision making when doctors move away from the absolute of "do no harm"[2] to other standards. The oldest way of making ethical decisions, represented by the Hippocratic Oath as well as by Judeo-Christian thought, is to claim there are absolutes that cannot be violated. Whether spelled out in the Ten Commandments or in a code such as the Hippocratic Oath or simply inscribed on the human heart, the truth of "thou shalt not kill" has until recently been universally accepted.

In specific cases of medical ethics, however, quoting an absolute is often no longer enough. It is one thing to say "do not kill," but it's not so easy to apply the words amid the complexity of modern medical technology. For example, the person who refuses medical intervention because of a cultural abhorrence for "life support" may not recognize that as unjustified neglect or as killing. On the other hand, to insist that all technological possibilities must be used may be refusing to allow an irretrievably terminal patient to die in peace. Put another way, the parishioner who argues "I want everything done" may be as inappropriate as the one who argues "I want nothing done."

Sad to say, ethical decisions today are commonly made, not by following absolutes such as "thou shalt not kill" but by giving in to the pull of sentimentality and "feel good" ethics that urge, "If it feels right, it must be right." Ours is not an age of deep thinkers, and technological advancement does not imply wisdom in the use of what we create or how we use it. The best-intentioned doctors and patients may sometimes make decisions based not on well-thought reasons but on the basis of sentimental impulses.

Furthermore, broad interpretation of civil rights today has all but eliminated reason altogether and has promoted sentimentality in place of all absolutes. A family member feeling his way through an ethical dilemma may not seek the insightful advice of others, but instead may rely upon what he has learned from television talk shows (entertainment in the guise of knowledge). Without a solid tradition of medicine and faith to guide him, today's decision maker often thinks he is liberated when in reality he is abiding by the shallow norms reflected in media sensationalism and sentimentality. Pastors have a challenge to alert parishioners to the uniqueness of the Christian life and faith in the face of such media propaganda.

The Hippocratic Oath has been side-stepped also by simple "expediency." If a patient is suffering, it's "expedient" to remove food and water in order to end the suffering through death—even when the patient is not otherwise dying. Or, if in order to care for a sick person, a life of hardship is anticipated, the "expedient" choice might be made to end the life. On rare occasions, avoidance of suffering and hardship may play some minor role in choice of treatment, but expedience can never justify intentionally killing anyone.

Finally, a dangerously subtle and foolish influence on decision making might simply be called "being nice." This attitude relies not upon absolutes nor sentimentality nor expediency, but appeals to what is temptingly called "common decency"—as in, "We put animals to sleep; why not humans?" Some who want to be open-minded claim that the decision to end the life of another is at times only "common sense" in the light of all they've been through. I recall a nurse asking, "Why are they letting this person live?" It is a careless attitude. Intolerance for suffering, our own or the patient's, pressures us to be done with it and to get on with our own life. While one can sympathize with this frustration, it remains a sin to dismiss others as burdens to be disposed of, even in the name of "being nice" to them.

THEOLOGY OF THE CROSS: A CHRISTIAN ETHIC

Christians stand at a crossroads in medical ethics. Faced with the option of choosing death at the hands of a morally deteriorating society, Christians must choose life at the foot of the cross. Patient rights, the financial burden of caring for someone, and quality of life casuistry—all arguments for ending a life—should not be convincing for the Christian who wants to do what is right and faithful in the eyes of God. The Christian's basis for decision making is an understanding of who we are, what life means, and how God relates to us. Our values, beliefs, and morality grow out of everything God tells us about human sinfulness, the need for redemption, and the promise that all things work for the good of those who love God.

It is not surprising that at the center of our individualistic, relativistic, and utilitarian world is the fear of finding ourselves helpless and without control over our lives in illness or as we grow old.

This fear of helplessness, played upon by the sensation-seeking media, portrays the medical profession as sadistically enjoying our helplessness for its own advantage.

In response to the fear of helplessness, our culture has produced Living Wills and the Durable Power of Attorney for Health Care, believing we have solved in advance the possibility of being found helpless in times of illness. Medical Directives are not bad in themselves, but their appeal to fears of helplessness and lack of control have to be critiqued. A promotional video produced by a bioethics center assures the participant, "The viewer is led to see that executing a health care treatment directive along with a Durable Power of Attorney is one of the most life-affirming actions that anyone can take, because it gives the individual control of his/her life to its very end."[3] The temptation to take charge of our lives must be identified for what it is: sin, "for when you [do], you will be like God."[4] A better idea is to entrust our lives to God, especially in helpless moments. Living at the foot of the cross reminds us that, precisely when we are helpless and must admit our loss of control over life, God reveals himself to us and reshapes us. "While we were yet [helpless]," Paul writes, "at the right time Christ died for the ungodly."[5]

Fear of helplessness is the last thing Christians need to fear. We feed on helplessness and live by grace. Ultimately, the obedience of faith is to submit to God in our helplessness and to trust him no matter what the outcome. Jesus promises, "He who loses his life [the self] for my sake will find it."[6] Losing ourselves in Christ transforms us from victims into witnesses. By our willingness to live with suffering, we testify to the truth that "You are not your own; you were bought with a price. [Therefore] glorify God in your body."[7]

Christ's suffering on the cross hid his glory. Similarly, the glory we give God in our suffering is also hidden—though very real. We may be asking, "Where is God when I need him?" I have seen patients who are crushed by the silence that follows this question stop praying, claiming they have lost faith. They believe they are experiencing Jesus' abandonment when he cried, "My God, my God, why have you forsaken me?"

To the question "Where is God when I need him," the theology of the cross answers, "He is on the cross, where you need him most. There Jesus fulfilled God's promise for you: 'Neither death, nor life ... nor anything else ... will be able to separate us from the love of God in Christ Jesus our Lord.'[8] There we discover that 'in all things God works for the good of those who love him and who have been called according to his purpose.' "[9]

In summary, we are called to live in faithfulness to God in our illnesses and sufferings. We are to use whatever medical means God gives us to secure life; though when medical offerings can provide only limited help or may even add to our suffering, it may be acceptable to withdraw treatment and simply keep the dying person comfortable in his dying. Hospices offer this comfort. It is important, however, for the Christian to object to any action that intentionally aims at death. Waiting patiently for death to come becomes an act of faith. It is not as though nothing is happening when the Christian waits. While we wait for the Lord to act, God is working with the circumstances of our lives to do what is good and right for us. We walk by faith, not by sight, and "so we do not lose heart. Though our outer nature is wasting away, our inner nature is being renewed every day."[10]

THE FUNCTION OF THE PASTOR IN ETHICAL DECISION MAKING

Many pastors may feel inadequate for face-to-face discussions with a doctor or an ethicist who knows a vocabulary and technology the pastor has never heard. But even if ignorant of clinical technology or the language of ethics, no pastor ought to claim inability, disinterest, or unwillingness to think theologically. Study of Holy Scripture and an acknowledgment of church history and the cumulative wisdom of the faithful form the foundation for making the connection between our Lord Jesus Christ and medical ethics. Furthermore, subscribing to the ethic of the theology of the cross places pastors in an important, critical minority position in discussions of ethical dilemmas.

Providing care to patients and families facing ethical dilemmas requires that the pastor function as advocate, clarifier, communicator, and truth-sayer. In these ways the pastor will be of great help in determining if dilemmas are real or imagined.

142

A true ethical dilemma confronts a person with difficult choices, but choices he can live with either way. An imagined ethical dilemma identifies options that are, in fact, not options at all for the faithful Christian. For example, a real dilemma exists in choosing between (a) administering pain relievers that may unintentionally shorten life or (b) allowing a person to suffer pain and live longer. This kind of a dilemma may be resolved through advocacy, clarification of medical implications, better communication between doctor and patient, or truth-saying. An imagined ethical dilemma is the choice between life or intentionally aiming at one's own or another's death (as in physician-assisted suicide or euthanasia). Because killing oneself or another person is not an option for Christians, the Christian need not see this as an ethical dilemma to be faced, much less decided. God has made that decision for us.

Some dilemmas are man-made when we focus on the wrong questions. In avoidance of the real issue of faithfulness, focus shifts to a peripheral issue such as the debate about *who* has the right to choose rather than *what* is chosen. (It is difficult for unbelievers to understand that Christians would rather choose to live with suffering than choose death at their own or another's hand.)

The Pastor as Advocate

One role the pastor may serve is that of an advocate for the patient. Although the function of advocacy is probably more prophetic (teaching) than pastoral (nurturing), the pastor at times must function in defense of the weak and helpless. His role is not to force his way on adversaries but to teach and speak peaceably on the patient's or family's behalf. My encounter with Maggie's physician in the hallway was such an attempt. More likely, the pastor will find his physical arena of advocacy in the Intensive Care lounge, if he can be present when discussion occurs between parishioner and doctor. The pastor can gently raise the right questions or pose options not yet thought of by either party. Advocacy need not turn into an adversarial relationship with either doctor or parishioner. Advocacy is especially useful when the patient and/or family is not strong or verbally skilled enough to be able to say what needs to be said. As an advocate, the pastor, speaking to the doctor, might say something like, "I think what Mrs. So-and-so is trying to say is ..."

The Pastor as Clarifier

Another way the pastor can help when people are facing real ethical dilemmas is to function as a clarifier. There have been times when, after sitting with a family member confronted by an ethical dilemma, I have asked, "What did *you* hear the doctor saying?" In one case, the wife of a patient replied, "He said that if my husband doesn't have this surgery, he will die." Actually, what the doctor said was, "If he doesn't have this surgery, he will be in a wheelchair the rest of his life." In the mind of this patient's wife, both statements were synonymous. Sometimes what appears as an ethical dilemma is really a problem of misunderstanding.

If the patient or family tells the doctor they want the pastor included in their family conferences at the hospital, the pastor will have an opportunity to be a helpful observer who can add clarity to the situation. Clarification may be needed, for example, in understanding terms such as "brain dead," "artificial feeding," or "heroic measures"—emotionally-loaded terms frequently used to persuade rather than to clarify. The doctor who refers to his patient as a "vegetable" rather than as a severely disabled person implies that the patient would be better off dead than alive. In as face-saving a way as possible, the pastor might want to call this to the doctor's attention in the parishioner's presence. Doctors too are affected by popular negative attitudes toward the handicapped or disabled, and sometimes think the patient or family would not want someone to live with disability. More than once I have heard a doctor say, "I wouldn't want my mother to live that way," implying that anyone who does is cruel. The pastor's task of clarification is crucial.

The Pastor as Communicator

Whereas the pastor's task as clarifier is primarily aimed at helping the patient or family understand the doctor, the pastor's function as communicator is aimed at helping the doctor understand the patient. For example, a doctor may ask "What do you want us to

144

do" and pose options in which the meaning, intent, and ethical implications are often unclear. Rather than selecting the next move from the physician's menu of proposed options, a family member might well state clearly, "I want you to do what is good. If the patient is dying and there is little or no hope of recovery, then I want you to keep him comfortable, but do nothing to cause death." This hands responsibility back to the physician where I believe it belongs, yet sets limits on the doctor's actions. Since most families do not think clearly in times of stress, the pastor may help communicate this message. The pastor does not deliver it himself, but coaches the family member to do so.

The pastor might also help the family think of new options, taking into account family differences of opinion. Two sisters, concerned with doing the right thing for a third sister, were at odds. One wanted nothing more done for her dying sister, and the other wanted everything done. In discussion with them I discovered the underlying reasons for each of their views. One sister wanted everything done because she did not want to be the cause of her sister's death. The other wanted nothing done because she did not want to put her sister through more suffering than she had already experienced. Both sisters had legitimate concerns. Since the sister was dying, I suggested that nothing new be introduced and that present treatment be continued. In this way, any chance of recovery was supported, while leaving her life in the hands of God. They accepted this solution. Together the three of us then met with the nurse, who communicated the decision to the doctor. The doctor was agreeable to their decision and appreciative of my intervention.

The Pastor as Truth-Sayer

Yet another role the pastor plays is that of truth-sayer. There is a growing acceptance of death in our time as something natural and even fulfilling. Those who accept this presupposition find it easier to choose death even when life is a viable option. To see death simply as something natural is naive and ignores the flaw of human nature which Christians call sinful. Furthermore, deception often accompanies this presupposition. For example, people talk of "allowing" a person to die, when what they mean is "causing" the person to die. In the accepted belief that suffering renders life meaningless, death is proposed as treatment.

The pastor as truth-sayer brings Good News in Jesus Christ. The pastor reminds the suffering person that Christian presuppositions are different from the world's, and that there is a critical distinction between death as the *result* of our choices and death as the *aim* of our choices. If the doctor offers treatment that results in death, that is tragic. If he offers treatment that aims at death as the outcome, that is sin.

The pastor as truth-sayer can also help the parishioner evaluate the choice of further treatment by using Gil Meilaender's criteria of "futility" and "burden."[11] *Futile* treatment is treatment that is available but provides little or no medical benefit to the patient. However, wherever medical treatment is sustaining the life of a patient (as in tube-feeding a viable but disabled person), it is not medically futile to do so. It may indeed be that no one would want to live this way, but faithfulness means living whatever life God gives.

Treatment that is a *burden* refers to treatment that increases suffering, making the treatment more a burden than the illness. Such burdensome treatment might legitimately, but not necessarily, be rejected. This would not always apply however to treatment that could successfully reverse a terminal condition. Treatment that causes severe physical or emotional distress may sometimes be rejected, not as a rejection of life but as a rejection of pain. For example, a patient who has undergone multiple surgeries yet who is terminally ill may finally choose to reject all further surgery because of physical or emotional depletion, hoping simply to live the life God has given until God decides otherwise.

The pastor's task of truth-saying will be most importantly that of pronouncing absolution for less-than-perfect (sinful) motivations. Even the best of choices may be made for less than the best of reasons. Christian morality is not based on our having done the right thing but on God's having done the right thing for us in Jesus Christ. We do not want to make light of the responsibility we have in the face of ethical decision making at the end of life. God encourages us to act boldly in the face of choices that are less than ideal, knowing we live by grace.

The pastor's most difficult task is to convince the sufferer of sin, inviting the sufferer to confess, for example, his anger at his wife's well-intentioned but inept care of him, or his manipulation of the nurses or his unreconciled relationship with God. It ought not be physical suffering that crushes but the realization of sin. Then healing brought by the pastor's words of forgiveness are a light in the darkness of the suffering person's life.

Epilog: Under the Cross

In the preceding pages I have tried to offer not so much a theory of pastoral care as my own practice and theology of pastoral care. First, I defined pastoral care as "the uninvited nurturing of those suffering some kind of helplessness and loss of control over their lives." The uninvited aspect emphasizes the pastor's initiative rather than the sufferer's in addressing suffering. The pastor has an invitation from God, if not from the patient. By virtue of the pastor's calling from Christ, he enters the lives of suffering people and helps them discover, by way of the cross, victory for their broken lives. Jesus, who died and has risen, provides healing for the inner person and gives life in the midst of death.

Competing with this definition of spiritual care, pop psychology's preoccupation with self-care has deterred many from reaching beyond themselves to care for others. Christian self-care is called repentance. It pays attention to the need for the cross in each believer's life as the starting place for extending care to others who are suffering.

The premise of this book is that it is not the task of pastoral care to eliminate suffering but to help suffering people interpret their suffering from the perspective of the cross. The cross not only assures our eternal salvation, but it also provides life in this vale of tears. Recently, after hearing me say this, a pastor told me, "My parishioners are affluent and healthy; they don't have any suffering in their lives." My first response was thankfulness that I was not one of that pastor's parishioners, since he obviously was not sensitive to their hurts nor in touch with their lives. Next, I tried to help him see that the cross addresses anxieties and fears that plague all of us and that suffering is more than physical pain and poverty. Every pastor ought to be able to see in each parishioner's life the need for pastoral care. To do this he must know them.

EPILOG: UNDER THE CROSS

The permeating theme of this book is the theology of the cross, articulated by Martin Luther in his Heidelberg Disputation of 1518. There the Reformer emphasizes God's redeeming presence and loving kindness in the midst of all suffering, whether it is the Lord's suffering or ours. The cross is the focal point of our redemption and the paradigm for living faithfully in the midst of suffering. In antithesis to the theology of the cross, the theology of glory views the Christian faith as a tool to accomplishing great things, not the least of which is the overcoming of all suffering. Faith, according to the theology of glory, is a utilitarian means to health, wealth, and success, a faith that sees no place for Christ in the midst of suffering, either his or ours. However, the Christian faith is not a tool to this end but a caring arm extended to the suffering. If God gives healing here and now, good and well. If not, he will in the end. Meanwhile, it is the task of Christian caregivers to walk with people in their suffering and to point them to the cross, where they find healing for the inner person, even though the outer person may be wasting away.

What makes the theology of the cross absolutely essential in pastoral care is the danger each person faces who attempts to take matters of suffering and helplessness into his own hands and out of the hands of God. This is not to say that suffering ought be allowed to continue where obvious and faithful ways to remove or alleviate it are available, but this is primarily the calling of doctors, nurses, social workers, therapists, counselors, and others who attempt to remove pain and suffering. Pastoral care, in contrast, focuses not on the removal of suffering but on bearing one another's burdens and pointing the sufferer to the cross.

Although I have written primarily for pastors, much here applies to all Christians in their bearing of one another's sufferings. Laypeople who offer spiritual care to suffering people need to develop the same sensitivity and skills that pastors should display. Both pastor and lay caregiver also need to pay attention to their own repentance and sufferings and find peace with God personally before ministering to others. Otherwise they will become wooden and insensitive, or they will succumb to the theology of glory and try to make others better rather than sharing suffering in the name of

Christ and helping people entrust their lives to God, who gives peace and healing according to his will.

Acknowledgment of the inevitability of suffering in this life is prerequisite to addressing suffering rightly. If the naive belief that we can remove all suffering from life becomes our aim as spiritual caregivers, we will end up in sympathy with those who propose eliminating suffering by eliminating sufferers by means of suicide or euthanasia. If, on the other hand, we see that life will always be filled with suffering, we will embrace our calling to bear our own sufferings or to help others bear theirs in Christ's name.

I have applied the theology of the cross to spiritual care of the elderly, those with AIDS, the dying and mourners, those with mental illness (especially depression), and to the complex field of medical ethics. In all of these situations the ultimate goal is to help the sufferer learn to live faithfully in the midst of suffering and to entrust his or her life to God, where peace is found and where healing takes place. The most challenging aspect of this is to be found in the current debates about medical ethics. The underlying issue in the current debate about medical ethics is fear of helplessness and loss of control. These fears cause sufferers and their families to abandon faith in God and to follow the lead of those who urge them to "take control of their lives." Perhaps the subject of medical ethics deserves a closer examination from the perspective of the theology of the cross. Meanwhile, the last chapter of this book will have to suffice as a starting place.

ENDNOTES

Preface

1. Martin Luther, "Heidelberg Disputation," *Luther's Works*: Volume 31 (Philadelphia: Muhlenberg Press. 1957), 52. Hereafter, *Luther's Works* are designated *LW*.

Part 1

Introduction: The Context of Pastoral Care Today

1. Pandit Rajmani Tigunait, "Spiritual Unfoldment and Total Well-Being," a seminar sponsored by the Himalayan International Institute of Yoga Science and Philosophy, R. R. 1, Box 400, Honesdale, PA 18431.
2. Andrea Frank, "Soothing the Soul," a weekend retreat sponsored by the Spiritual Wellness Network, 523 N. 66th Avenue, Wauwatosa, WI 53213-4057.
3. Richard C. Eyer, "The Psychologizing of Life and Faith," *Lutheran Forum*, Advent 1984.

Chapter 1. The Cross as Paradigm for Pastoral Care

1. *LW*, 31, 52.
2. Ibid.
3. 1 Corinthians 1:18 RSV.
4. *LW*, 31, 55.
5. Ibid., 52.
6. Ibid., 53.
7. 2 Corinthians 12:9 NIV.
8. Gene Edward Veith, *Reading Between The Lines: A Christian Guide to Literature*. (Wheaton, Illinois: Crossway Books, 1990), 103.
9. Ibid., 104–5.
10. Ibid.

Chapter 2. The Pastor as Cross-Bearer

1. William E. Hulme, *Your Pastor's Problems* (Minneapolis: Augsburg Publishing House), 45.
2. Paul Tournier, *The Strong and The Weak* (Philadelphia: The Westminster Press), 97.
3. Ibid., 97.
4. Ibid., 131.
5. *LW*, 31, 53.
6. 1 Timothy 3: 4–5 NIV.

Chapter 3. Sickness, Suffering, and the Cross

1. 1 Corinthians 11:27–30.
2. Harold S. Kushner, *When Bad Things Happen To Good People* (New York: Avon Books, 1981).
3. Stanley Hauerwas, *Naming The Silences* (Grand Rapids: William B. Eerdmans Publishing Co. 1990), 2.
4. Dietrich Bonhoeffer, *Meditating On The Word* (New York: Ballantine Book, 1986), 86.
5. *The Wholistic Health Center*, a brochure produced by the Wholistic Health Centers, Inc., 137 South Garfield Street, Hinsdale, Illinois 60521.
6. C. S. Lewis, *Surprised by Joy: The Shape of My Early Life* (New York: Harcourt, Brace and Company, 1968), 229.

Chapter 4. Faith, Healing, and the Cross

1. John 14:6 NIV.
2. Revelations 21:3–4 RSV.
3. Luke 4:34 NIV.
4. Luke 5:17–26 NIV.
5. John 9:2–3 RSV.

Part 2: The Cross in Action: Practical Pastoral Care in Specific Circumstances

1. *Lutheran Worship*, (St. Louis: Concordia Publishing House, 1982).
2. Ibid., 136.
3. Ibid., 136.
4. Ibid., 139.
5. Ibid., 140.
6. Ibid., 145.

7. Ibid., 149.

8. Ibid., 153.

9. Ibid., 155.

10. John 19:26–27 RSV.

11. Matthew 1:23.

12. Matthew 1:21.

13. Nicene Creed.

14. John 20:28 NIV.

15. Matthew 9:21 RSV.

16. Eugene H. Peterson, *Five Smooth Stones for Pastoral Work* (Atlanta: John Knox Press, 1980).

Chapter 5. Crossing the Years: The Elderly

1. C. S. Lewis, *Letters of C. S. Lewis* (New York and London: Harcourt Brace Jovanovich, 1975), 308.

2. Erik H. Erikson, *Childhood and Society* (New York: W. W. Norton & Company, Inc., 1986) and Daniel J. Levinson, *The Seasons of a Man's Life* (New York: Ballantine Books, 1986).

3. Romans 5:3–5 RSV.

4. Romans 5:6 RSV.

5. 2 Corinthians 12:9 RSV.

Chapter 6. With the Aid of the Cross: AIDS

1. "AIDS" is shorthand for the *Acquired* (not inherited) *Immune Deficiency* (a breakdown of the body's defense system, producing susceptibility to certain diseases) *Syndrome* (a spectrum of disorders and symptoms). People with the full-blown form of AIDS suffer from unusual, life-threatening infections and/or rare forms of cancer.
The virus that causes AIDS also produces milder but often debilitating illnesses as part of what is called AIDS-Related Complex, or ARC.
The virus that causes AIDS and AIDS-related conditions is now called Human Immunodeficiency Virus (HIV). HIV is a retrovirus that must live and reproduce inside human cells. It is extremely fragile and does not survive long outside the body.

2. *Christianity Today*, April 8, 1988, 36.

3. *Christianity Today*, April 8, 1988, 37.

Chapter 7. On the Cross: Dying

1. Peter Kreeft, *Love Is Stronger Than Death* (San Francisco: Ignatius Press, 1992), 22.

2. Ibid.

3. Ibid., 23.
4. 1 Thessalonians 4:14.
5. Romans 6:3–4 RSV.
6. Romans 6:6 RSV.
7. Colossians 3:3 RSV.

Chapter 8. At the Foot of the Cross: Mourners

1. Colin Murray Parkes, *Bereavement, Studies of Grief in Adult Life* (New York: International Universities Press Inc., 1979).
2. Granger E. Westberg, *Good Grief,* (Philadelphia, Pa., Fortress Press, 1978).
3. 1 Thessalonians 4:13 RSV.
4. Martin Luther, *Day By Day We Magnify Thee* (Philadelphia: Augsburg Fortress, 1982), 18.
5. 1 Thessalonians 4:17–18 RSV.

Chapter 9. Crossing the Line: Mental Illness

1. *Lutheran Worship* (St. Louis: Concordia Publishing House, 1982), 201.
2. Martin Luther, *The Small Catechism* (St. Louis: Concordia Publishing House, 1986), 22–23.

Chapter 10. Feeling Crossed Out: Depression

1. 2 Corinthians 4:8–9 NIV.
2. Luke 11:24–26 NIV.
3. *Letters of C. S. Lewis,* Edited with a memoir by W. H. Lewis (New York: Harcourt, Brace, and World Book, 1966), 241.
4. John 17:15 NIV.
5. 1 Corinthians 6:19–20 NIV.
6. Isaiah 45:15 RSV.
7. *LW,* 31, 51.

Chapter 11. At the Crossroad: Medical Ethics

1. Hippocratic Oath.
2. Ibid.
3. "Living Choices" brochure (Urbana, Illinois: Carle Media, n.d.).
4. Genesis 3:5 RSV.

5. Romans 5:6 RSV.
6. Matthew 10:39 RSV.
7. 1 Corinthians 6:19–20 RSV.
8. Romans 8:38–39 RSV.
9. Romans 8:28 NIV.
10. 2 Corinthians 4:16 RSV.
11. Gilbert Meilaender, "Ethical Decision Making at the End of Life," a paper presented at Doctor/Clergy Clinic Day, Columbia Hospital, December 6, 1991.